Nectar of Nondual Truth

CONTENTS

10 Essence of Advaita Vedanta, Part 2
by Alexander Hixon
In this second installment of three, more of the deep nondual elements of Gaudapada's commentary on the Mandukyopanisad are revealed for contemplation.

16 Ladder of Spiritual Ascent in Jainism
by Swami Brahmeshananda
This is the ninth in an ongoing series of articles on the Jain religion, gleaned from the first hand experience of this swami of the Ramakrishna Order who lived and learned among the Jains while on pilgrimage to their holy sites and temples.

20 The Gunas in Vedic Cosmology
by Annapurna Sarada
The teaching of the three gunas of Prakriti, unique in all the philosophies of the world, bears repeating many times in order that it sink into the human mind on a primal level, revealing the need to transcend all three and break free of the bondage of cycles they sustain.

27 Mumukshutvam – Desire for Freedom
by Babaji Bob Kindler
In Vedanta, one gains the pure desire for Liberation from rock solid faith. This faith springs from the ability to concentrate the mind on Reality, which in turn proceeds from qualities such as forbearance, contentment, inner peace, and self control. All of these are based in the ability to discriminate between what is essential and nonessential, followed by the successful move to detach from the nonessential at will.

32 Essentials of Judaism
by Rabbi Rami Shapiro
In a tour-de-force expose of the many facets of Judaism, the mainstays of a Jewish man's and woman's spiritual life and practice come to light, guiding the contemporary votary to a clear understanding of this ancient pathway to Enlightenment.

38 The Ecstatic Dissolution of the Self
by Anam Thubten Rinpoche
The marked difference, in both capacity and clarity of awareness, between the human ego and what realized souls speak of as Witness Consciousness, is well documented in this engaging article, transmitted from the enlightened perspective of Tibetan Buddhism by one of its dedicated Rinpoches. The entire premise of the teachings centers around gaining the ability in practice to gently let go of all egoic superimpositions in order to alleviate fear and embrace subtle joy within.

42 Requisites to Samadhi
by Swami Aseshananda
This is the ninth transcription of the many discourses of Swami Aseshananda that the Nectar staff has rendered for the written page, in service of the spiritual practitioner of Vedanta, as well as any lover of Truth and Philosophy. In this offering, the revered swami astutely lays out the necessary qualifications that a sincere aspirant will have to meet in order to place the soul in the superlative position for the rarest of all spiritual experiences — Samadhi.

47 Birth, Death, and the Bardo Plane
by Abbot Kyogen Carlson
Abbot Kyogen Carlson, Godo of the Dharma Rain Zendo in Portland, Oregon, departed the body in September of 2014. Prior to his demise he gave this talk on a subject that is seldom taken up in any depth in the Zen tradition, that of the Bardo state and its various planes. Necessarily — and poignantly, considering his own passing — this topic bridges on the inscrutable areas of human birth and death, a teaching that is extremely important to all schools of Buddhism.

"....only a well-rounded spiritual seeker will be able to reach a truly nondual state of Awareness, and this versatile soul attains to that incomparable status via contemplating and absorbing the enlightened realizations of the sages, saints, seers, and saviors of all religions."

Publisher's Page

Sarada Ramakrishna Vivekananda – SRV Associations
"Setting the feet of humanity on the path of Universal Truth."

Notes on an Advaitic Journal

At the basis of Advaita as the philosophy of Shankara and his gurus, there is Advaita as experience. Advaita as experience represents that supreme place where all diversity merges in its Essence. It is not combatant or immiscible with qualified or dualistic approaches, but rather provides them their place of consummate arrival. Where actual practice rather than mere book learning is emphasized, where religion, philosophy and spirituality are not separate from one another, where knowledge and love, reason and devotion, are never divorced from each other, there does the truth of authentic nonduality effloresce.

Historically speaking, experiential Advaita originated with the ancient Rishis. Therefore, the Upanisads contain the nondual truths of the Vedas which declare: idam mahabhutam anantam aparam vijnanaghana eva, *"This great Being is endless and without limit. It is a mass of indivisible Consciousness only."*

SRV Associations & Universality

The SRV Associations are part of a worldwide movement of spiritual aspirants devoted to the study and practice of Vedanta and Divine Mother Wisdom. The ideals of this ancient pathway to God, exemplified in the lives of Sri Sarada Devi, Sri Ramakrishna and Swami Vivekananda, are the original and eternal perfection of the Soul and its inherent oneness with Reality, the manifesting of divinity in our lives, selfless service of all beings as God, and reverence for the ultimate unity of all sacred traditions. To this end our purpose is to study, worship, and contemplate Truth so that spirituality may flourish. This is the Advaitic way — *"None else but Self, none other than Mother."*

Nectar's Mission — Advaita-Satya-Amritam

In Sanskrit, *amrita*, nectar also means Immortality – and this is, indeed, what we are offering: opportunities to become aware of this Amrita that is our very Essence via the rarefied teachings from Vedanta and the World Religions and Philosophies that appear in each issue of Nectar.

Nectar of Non-Dual Truth is SRV Associations' heartfelt offering of highest Wisdom to the human community. It is the sincerest form of love and service we know to disseminate nondual Truth and teachings which transmit pure knowledge, pure love, and true universality. Through Nectar we are working out SRV's mission of spiritual upliftment and education. Please join us; this is a universal movement.

Keeping Nectar in Print

Nectar is a free magazine that can be ordered in printed form online at www.srv.org, and it can also be viewed online. (play.google.com/books) However, substantial donations are needed every year to maintain this publication in print. Why is this important?

1 – Printed Nectars are best for person to person and organization to organization dissemination of these ennobling teachings that deepen one's own spiritual life and engender knowledge of, acceptance, and reverence for all other paths.

2 – Only printed copies can reach those who do not have access to online viewing, including prison inmates, who are a particular focus of SRV's social seva.

Use the subscription/donation form provided at the back of this issue to send a check or credit card payment to SRV Associations, P.O. Box 1364, Honokaa, HI., 96727, or donate online at www.srv.org. Your donations are tax deductible.

With reverent gratitude, we heartily thank the contributing writers of this issue of Nectar of Nondual Truth, who have so graciously and selflessly shared the wisdom of their respective traditions and practices.

Staff of Nectar of Nondual Truth

Publisher
Sarada Ramakrishna Vivekananda Associations
an Annual Publication
For more information concerning the SRV Associations or Nectar of Nondual Truth please contact:
SRV Associations, PO Box 1364, Honoka'a, HI 96727
Phone: (808) 990-3354
e-mail: srvinfo@srv.org   website: www.srv.org
Nectar Subscription is on a donation basis only

No part of this publication may be reproduced or transmitted in any form without permission from the publisher. Entire contents copyright 2015. All Rights Reserved. ISSN 1531-1414

Editor
Babaji Bob Kindler

Associate Editor
Annapurna Sarada

Production
Lokelani Kindler

Acknowledgement
*Image of Ramakrishna's Disciples
Courtesy of Vedanta Press*
800-816-2242

Cover Image:
Swift Current Lake

Contributing Writers
Swami Aseshananda
Swami Brahmeshananda
Dr. Alexander Hixon
Anam Thubten Rinpoche
Abbot Kyogen Carlson
Annapurna Sarada
Rabbi Rami Shapiro
Babaji Bob Kindler

EDITORIAL

    Judaism, Jainism, Tibetan Buddhism, Zen Buddhism, Vedanta, and Advaita Vedanta, are all represented in full in this issue of Nectar of Nondual Truth, *and if we had the available pages and writers we would certainly include all the rest of the world's religious traditions herein as well. For, The Religion of the coming age, and of all ages — recognized as such or not — is Universality, and its underlying essence is Nonduality (advaita). Different liquids may be pleasing to the palate, but only water really slakes our thirst. Similarly, religion brings solace to embodied souls, but only nonduality slakes the inner thirst of the soul yearning to be free. Odors of cooked food wafting on the air bring children running for their meal, but only eating it truly satisfies their hunger. Like this, the inward fragrance of religion attracts the soul to perform worship and meditate, but only merging with Divine Reality fulfills all their aims and ends. The holy water and sacred food of the soul, then, is Universality based in Nonduality.*

    Universality is beyond interreligious harmony and outstrips eclecticism. It breathes free, grows, and expands in the rare and exalted atmosphere of the open mind of the sincere and dedicated aspirant. Like the headiness of breathless heights one feels on pilgrimage in the Himalayan mountains, or the inspiration felt by taking pilgrimage to Jerusalem, or the power present when going on Hajj to Mecca, just so Universality verily transports the human mind to lofty experiences of Consciousness felt nowhere else — not even in the life heavens or the causal realms!

    This rarefied trans-philosophical status called Universality is really not all that uncommon; all beings know of it and feel it somewhere in themselves. Even within the pages of our own English dictionary one can find its superlative sentiments. If several of these dictionaries are consulted, and an amalgam is fashioned from their various definitions, we find this expression as the result: "Universality is a principle corresponding to reality and its essence which declares that all beings will be saved based upon a truth that is comprehensively broad and versatile, existent and operative everywhere and under all conditions, that embraces the totality of mankind without limits or exceptions regardless of religious differences, and that is easily adaptable or adjustable to meet the varied philosophical requirements of all of humanity."

    It is no wonder, then, that Swami Vivekananda brought to us and championed this unique perspective in the West, and to the world at large in recent times. As he was wont to say, taking the principle even beyond the pale of religious traditions: "We reject none — neither theist, pantheist, monist, polytheist, agnostic, nor atheist — the only condition of being a disciple is modeling a character at once the broadest and most intense. We leave everybody free to know, select, and follow whatever suits and helps him."

    And this is what Nectar of Nondual Truth *is all about. Short of journals that may occasionally include a courtesy article of another religion in their pages,* Nectar *declares the equal status of all world religions and, not content with that, moves to display the teachings of every tradition, issue to issue. This allows the open-minded aspirant to actually study and learn from other religious perspectives — not just coming from a "sister religion," as one of the more liberal Catholic Popes once said — but as a reverent testament to the universal truths that exist in all world religions.*

    Furthermore, the reasoning behind this declares that only a well-rounded spiritual seeker will be able to reach a truly nondual state of Awareness, and this versatile soul attains to that incomparable status via contemplating and absorbing the enlightened realizations of the sages, saints, seers, and saviors of all religions.

    Therefore, it is not mere tolerance, as Mahatma Gandhi once said, but a thorough understanding of another's religious perspectives — including scriptural wisdom, techniques of practice, comprehension of rites and rituals, and even modes of specific worship, to name a few — that will constitute the actual practice and principle of Universality in action among spiritual seekers.

    Om Peace, Peace, Peace.

Babaji Bob Kindler

NECTAR OF ADVAITIC INSTRUCTION

Questions from Our Readers

Questions arising in the mind of a sincere aspirant, and answers flowing forth from the loving heart of the preceptor, create the salubrious atmosphere of peaceful, blissful resolution. In that space, the two become One.

"There has been a sort of impatience that has occured within me lately, but I think that will soon dissolve into daily sadhana. But what would you say to a person who thinks that 'Realization will come in time?'"

Realization will come in time; it is true. Though enlightenment is a principle always and ever at hand, it dawns on the mind in stages. This is called krama mukti, and must be allowed for so long as man is in an embodied state, especially here on the earth plane. Sadhana, your spiritual practice, is the qualifier there. Seekers must make certain that they are not just waiting for some hoped for grace, but are preparing the way for it. As Swami Vivekananda has quoted, *"Not he that crieth 'Lord, Lord,' but he that doeth the will of the Lord."* The world is full of hope, but there is precious little self-effort. This has led conventional religion to depend upon and advise the way of the savior rather than follow the noble path of the exemplar. As Sri Ramakrishna has so perfectly put it: *"The Wind of God's Grace is ever blowing, but one must raise one's sail to catch It."* Therefore, become a mariner of the Sea of Consciousness, i.e., be thou a yogi and practice spiritual disciplines.

"I am feeling more and more established in the dharma after the significant time in Holy Company this month. The teachings and spiritual atmosphere are infectious, and the mind's tendency to gravitate towards worldly thoughts and enjoyments is greatly diminishing. I can't believe how powerful of a tool svadhyaya is in this area. Can one do japa until formless meditation comes naturally, when the mind stops vibrating so much, or do I need to be sure and attempt formless meditation every day, no matter what?"

In our tradition, and particularly our lineage (Ramakrishna Order), japa is used to settle the mind so that it can meditate naturally, and without interference (chitta vrittis) on the formless Brahman. One should spend time exploring that state which comes when thoughts die away due to settling practices and their influence. This is a slow, gradual, refined art, and that goes for the states of mind that come with it. One should look towards developing all this over thirty to forty years, never stopping at any juncture with the premature conclusion that the Goal has been reached. Speaking about this meditation path, the Great Master stated, *"A bird must eventually come to rest on a branch,"* but in another bird analogy He declared that *"No matter how high a bird might fly, there are still higher atmospheres to reach."*

"Our time on retreat with you was precious to us, and I am grateful for it. In reading over my notes, however, I found confusion about the teachings on thought, word, and deed. I remember discussing it, but not the outcome. We usually hear that our thoughts are larger than us, and we are not accountable if we do not act on them. In fact, I think perhaps that was the outcome of the discourse. But in my notes it says, '....living in a state of inaction when thoughts, words, and deeds are one.' Not very good notes! Can you help?"

The two themes in your notes, in accord with the subject, are both correct. First, there is that yogic accomplishment, of the highest order, where one lives amidst the perfect synthesis of thought, word, and deed. That is a kind of sthiti samadhi, or a state of constant equilibrium. Perfect peace of mind, along with abiding contentment, are its qualities. It is attained by purification of the mind, senses, and body, via sadhana. Purity of act will then become natural. Meditation (mind), moderation (senses), and detachment (body) are its practices.

As to your first point, it is in this yuga (age) alone that thinking the evil deed has no consequence (karma), but acting upon it does. In other yugas, when mankind is not so ignorant and violent, that would not be the case. There, in these higher mental climes, even thinking bad thoughts would produce unsavory results. We know that even here and now, on earth, bad thoughts are not healthy, but that has more to do with one's day-to-day health and mood. Bad thoughts/vibrations will not necessarily "create" bad karma, but they lead us towards them, and make us susceptible to falls. It is when these bad thoughts give way to bad acts that karma, and samskaras, set in.

"My question is: what is the point of having children and life if it is just to let it all go in the end and realize that it all was never yours to begin with?"

Simply put, the purpose of this life, or any life on earth, is to realize God here, in the worst possible circumstances, where the Reality is covered over by many veils. In other words, it is not life, nor children, nor any changing thing, circumstance, or personality, that is the main point. Only the Reality counts. That Reality is ours eternally. The rest changes and passes, eternally. As even the Western poet wrote, *"Earth's shadows fly, heaven's light forever shines. Life, like a dome of many-colored glass, stains the white radiance of Eternity."* As the Great Master explained: *"If you put many zeros together on end, they add up to zero. But put a '1' in front of that line of zeros and you have a huge number."*

"Do the scriptures make any mention of a type of meditation nightmare that can occur? I was doing japa yesterday, after having one of those dreams where a scene from a violent movie I haven't watched or thought of in years gets reenacted. Some type of face or image appeared as I recited the mantra and rushed forwards and scared the hell out of me. It was overwhelming and I had to rest a few moments before continuing. How do I stay calm when this happens?"

Once your routine is established, all doubts and fears will be put in their place. Frustrations will give way to peace and transcendence. You should know that now that you have become a party to the Vedanta, life will transform itself. As Swami Vivekananda has said, *"Once the soul hears the Vedanta, all abracadabras fall away by themselves. This has been my uniform experience. Upon attaining a higher vision, the lower ones fall off naturally."* Give it all some more time to sink in, and simply place a wall of protection around yourself via sadhana at home, in private. And remember, too, that the appearance of "wrathful deities" is most often a good sign....

"I find myself getting really stressed out about school, work, and money. When things get tight, it's hard not to worry about money. Since it's summer, and I am not in class, I get really down on myself when I don't feel productive. This is when thoughts of school and work come into play. What is a good mindset I should have towards school, work, and money. When I think about it, I feel I can come up with some decent answers to my own questions, but it helps to talk to you about it and get your input."

Swami Vivekananda once uttered a funny but important thing around this matter. He said, *"Two persons went to see Lord Jagannath in the temple. One of them beheld the Deity, while the other only saw some trash that had been haunting his mind."* The difference between the two is right orientation. The former seeks God while living in the world, but the latter is mistaking the world for God. Since the world is not God (not until one is qualified to see it as God), all manner of angst arises in the latter.

Stress is one of the unnatural side-effects of life in the world today. Too much emphasis is placed upon monetary gain and success — what Sri Ramakrishna called name, fame, and gain. Try to underplay those things while still making life work for you. That is the real challenge and wisest attainment here on earth — to live just "under the radar" of society, politics, taxes, fundamentalist religion, and other worldly and unholy distractions — all of them seeking money through various types of violence and warfare. God/Mother, is our Only Refuge; all other refuges are false, and disappoint in the end. The yogi/yogini living in the world will work to reduce unwholesome effects like stress, worry, disappointment, excitement over unreal things, and matters of that ilk, for they lead to depression, then worse. Increase your subtle bliss instead via time well spent in spiritual occupations, and live freely.

"I'm noticing that although devotion gives me power to continue on the path, only jnana gives me peace. Maybe the devotional path gives peace when one is far along it, I don't know. But I'm seeing jnana gives it instantly. All I can say is, 'Ah what blessed peace!' In the face of death, in the face of everything — peace. The world fades to a distance as unreal the more I look inward to see who I am. It is 'out there', while I am here, 'inside,' stable, settled, quiet, with what looks like a core of joy way down deep just waiting to emerge. I certainly can say at this point that I was completely mistaken about jnana and the path of the jnani. It isn't at all what I thought it was. It is not the presumed spiritual suicide that many of the Vaishnavas imagine it to be."

Fundamentalists always take the narrow view. It is those who have been given the wide view, the universal view, the "catholic" view — like Vivekananda gives it in this age — who know that integration of the Yogas is the consummate way. No more one-sidedness for them anymore.

Jnana and Bhakti are the two wings of the bird. Karma is the bird's body, and meditation is its tail feathers. With all of these the bird gets off the ground and soars, going where it likes, freely. These four Yogas — what Sri Krishna teaches and calls *"Chaturdasya Yoga"* in the *Bhagavad Gita*, form both the way out of suffering and the way to God. So, narrow Vaishnavas — narrow anyone — have no ground to stand on here with their "one-size fits all" philosophies.

Sri Krishna also gives out the good news that jnanam is the supreme destroyer of ignorance, and the best purifier of all ills as well. He states: *"In all the worlds, Arjuna, there is no purifier like wisdom. The yogis realize this fact in time."* And it is in the *Narada Bhakti Sutras* that we find that devotion cannot destroy ignorance like wisdom does, not unless it is extremely intense.

In other words, with meek or mild devotion, people go on worshipping at churches and temples, go on reading scriptures at ashrams and at home, and meditate for years on a Reality that is missing its element of Love, but nothing in them really changes, and they do not change. Life goes on in the same vein, called "mundane human convention." To quote Swami Vivekananda about this unfortunate situation:

"In the world, all things are done by people guided like lifeless machines. There is no mental activity, no unfoldment of the heart, no vibration of life, no flux of hope; there is no strong stimulation of the will, no experience of keen pleasure, nor the contact of intense sorrow; there is no stir of inventive genius, no desire for novelty, no appreciation of new things. Clouds never pass from this mind, the radiant picture of the morning sun never charms this heart. It never even occurs to the mind if there is any better state than this; where it does, it cannot convince; in the event of conviction, effort is lacking; and even where there is effort, lack of enthusiasm kills it out."

These words are a perfect description of what is wrong with the world, and why the human race cannot and will not rise to its inherent divine status. A little real wisdom will change all that. Thus, the Jnana Yoga takes its place as the purifier and the destroyer. And after those tasks are accomplished it ushers the jnani to the realm of the seers, to the company of those who have come to know Divine Reality as being Nondual in Essence.

"How important is it to cultivate Samadarshitvam? Should one feel the same intimacy with every human being as he should feel with Ishvara? Would it consider the roles to be different, the reality to be One? For, say, should I look the same way at my shakti friend as I would upon the local butcher?"

The principle of Samadarshitvam is both an ideal and an observance, but it is carried on with a mind that has already achieved transcendence. Until the mind is in a nondual state, then, one should instead practice the four parikarmas — reverence for the holy ones, happiness for those who are successful, compassion for those who suffer, and indifference for the evil-minded. For, the highest of axioms, like, for instance, nondoership, are both very rare and reserved for those in samadhi.

For the rest, like practitioners, they have to act practically, so teachings like the parikarmas are given. We cannot indiscriminately mix the nondual with the dual, the worldly with the spiritual, the fully attained with those who are still striving for attainment. Otherwise, it would be both naive and immature, and we risk transgressing the Advaitic Truths.

If you would practice Samadarshitvam in yourself, then do not call yourself worthless compared to the Luminaries. The same Atman is in you that is in them. They have realized It more than you, however. So the solution is to get busy and get realized. That is Samadarshitvam in practice.

"Meditation and japa are going on fairly well. I am now trying to meditate in the night when I can't sleep. Bad dreams are a problem right now. They have been somewhat of a problem since I returned from retreat. If waking and dreaming states are both ephemeral, and deep sleep is more like reality, how much should I worry about very sad, violent, or sexual dreams? At what stage do these troubling dreams disappear? Could medications that help depression in the day be a problem in the night?"

As for dreams, in your case — being a devotee of Divine Mother — they are of little matter. You are just running them through the mind to see an end to them. The acts that caused them to be there are like colored threads, and your mind is a spool. These threads — white, red, and black — run off the spool in the same way they ran on to the spool, and you are presently feeling them run off due to your sadhana.

And the fact that you have taken teachings on the three states of awareness as taught by Gaudapada is a good sign. They are probably surfacing now in accord with you placing attention on teachings relating to them on retreat. Wait a while, give them little attention, and they will pass. If they persist, you might want to take a morning's meditation and concentrate on them specifically, to see if you can trace them and dissolve them.

"I was wondering if you can explain how being meek according to the teachings of Christ is different from being weak? Perhaps you might share an example differentiating between how a meek person would act versus a weak person. The dividing line is not clear to me, and it seems every time the occasion arises for standing up for oneself, I tend to worry about going overboard and then end up just doing nothing."

Definitions of words are crucial to understanding. It is not that there may be different definitions to words that is so much the problem, as there are always shades of meaning that can be transmitted and understood. It is more that specification needs to be given when speaking on or about them.

As far as the word "meek" goes, it is not a very good word in English to express what Christ was trying to convey. Peaceful, nonviolent, humble, even gentle — these would all be words that fall more in line with His emphasis.

So "weak" is not the reference here, to say the least. What is more, the whole flavor of the teaching needs to be rendered in the atmosphere of clarity. I believe that the teaching reads that the meek shall *"inherit the earth."* The world that the meek inherit would not be the same world that the violent and domineering beings are trying to gain. The world that gentle souls want is Nature as it is, and a world of dharmic actions where desires can be effectively fulfilled, and God can be realized more readily.

So I have brought up the meek and the strong here because the strong *are* the weak. Real strength is letting go of the world due to it being unreal, transitory — because *"man has no place to lay his head."* Therefore he renounces it (the world). It is the weak, who cling to it, making a show of strength, who clutch ignobly at shifting sands, to changing phenomena, to empty objects — to unownable lands and unclaimable riches.

So those two areas — the meek, and the strong who are the weak — I comment on here, in hopes that your understanding will be clarified thereby.

"With an intense enough sadhana, can anyone reach the Goal in a single life?"

With the right type and level of sadhana, the goal can be reached swiftly. Of the five types of ways that beings generally rely upon (see the latest Raja Yoga lesson) in spiritual life, sadhana is one of the two best. But let us be clear that without guidance, any path, way, or method can swiftly end in failure. And sadhana devoid of the real reason to be doing it – to realize God — may also become ineffective.

And the level of sadhana is important. That is, if one's sadhana consists of, say, merely fasting, then not much real growth can be made. In other words, a well-rounded sadhana is needed. You are fortunate that, early on in the push for illumination of mind, you have come to Vedanta, and to Swamiji — who along with His Great Master, were Kings and Champions of Sadhana.

"I find that if it's true that I love God, then I love God because God is beautiful and the source of beauty, on every scale, in every way — from the beauty of pine branches waving in the wind, to the beauty of Krishna's form, to the balanced, intellectual beauty of sublime mystical doctrines. I don't love God because God is good, or for any other reason than that God is beautiful, and the source of beauty. Is this really love of God? Can I say I love God when there's this 'because' attached to it? I'm finding this question disturbing, disturbing enough that it's eroding some of my enthusiasm for sadhana. God's beauty thrills me, truly, but if this is why I love God, can I truly say I love God?"

There are a host of reasons to love God, and any or all of them are valid. God's unsurpassable beauty (*sundara*) is one of them. In one list, The Six Treasures of the Godhead, He/She/It is described as having unlimited abundance, magnificent glory, irresistible strength, penetrating wisdom, natural renunciation, and awesome splendor. I think that the second and sixth of this list would fall under your category of beauty. But the list taken in its entirety is, well, beautiful, is it not?

Then there are the modes one might consider. What is God? Who is He? Is He a He? How should I think of That? It all makes for good contemplation, and participation in what the seers call increasing one's faith in and devotion for God.

Finally, and as one of my friends in the distant past once said, "I do not know what God is, but I love God." Perhaps that says it all. Then again, the mind in love with God experiences different moods — bhavas, seeded samadhis, etc. And there is always that singular unseeded Samadhi, too......

"I decided to start eating meat about six months ago and not struggle with the matter anymore. I feel better when I eat meat, calmer and more stable. The only problem I'm having is the old idea I've struggled with my whole life that I shouldn't eat meat. I've gone back and forth over this, feeling better and finding my finances more manageable when I eat meat, then struggling to go purer, with the results being that I always felt undernourished and didn't have enough money for food. Of course, Swamiji once said to 'eat meat and lots of it,' but that never seemed very popular advice in the Ramakrishna movement. Of course, you, as my guru, may disapprove, which will have its effect on me and probably send me back to the drawing board. But if I get no negative reprisal, then I can finally just forget the whole food problem. My continuing concern with this problem, and the sense of frustration I feel with it, is a definite impediment to my focus in meditation, so if I could just forget about the matter, that could be a very good thing."

About diet, you will find me quite lenient about meat eating in general, but personally uncompromising in the matter. That is, I would never take flesh in my diet, and only wish I had not had to do so the first 19 years of my life, growing up in the West. Since 20 I have given up all meat-eating, and have been far the better for it, on several levels. What are those levels? Healthier body, lighter karma, clearer conscience, physical longevity. So it works for me; I have found my way and my balance. In regard to foods, I am also an example to the world of how a yogic type of person can live free of unnecessary conventions, crusty habits, and the harming of animals. In addition to this, if one has some small means and some ingenuity, vegetarian food can be and is delicious to the palate. As some might say, it adds an entirely different dimension to the "culinary art."

But it is neither practical nor wise to force one's way on others. Ironically, I am a victim of reverse discrimination in this matter, for the meat-eating world has made it hard for the vegetarian to travel and subsist at the same time. Thankfully, due to the efforts and persistence of a few of us, we are beginning to see vegetarian options show up in eateries across the world, even at such places as airports!

But back to leniency, we must let people come to finer things, like cleaner diet, over time. In my way of thinking, blessing what one eats with mantra is far more important than what one eats. Food blessed in the right way will not poison the bloodstream, whereas even pure, nutritious food, if not blessed, and eaten carelessly, will conduce to poison in the system.

In your case, you have a good way, maybe without even knowing it. You eat meat, then give it up, in turns, when you feel directed to do so or not. Perhaps you ought to get rid of that insinuating feeling of guilt around the matter, and just do what is best for you — and know that continuous sadhana, alone, will make up for any karma that one may accrue by taking life and transferring vital force from one source into another via eating. My guru used to say, "A man must eat to live, not live to eat." One's attitude can either purify or spoil any act and situation. Then, karma of another kind sets in.

It is good to be sensitive around the matter, around all matters, but practicality is also necessary. After all, some vegetarians want you to give up things like eggs and cheese, as if we are rabbits instead of complicated human beings. The raw foods people, and the vegans, they too, are often over the top. Many of them, I have found, could use a good period of ingesting denser food in order to reset their bodies, re-balance their minds and fill out their physique. It takes a strong body to realize God.

I never heard Swamiji saying that one should "eat meat and lots of it", as you have quoted here. When did he say that? Tell me where is it cited? And in what context and to whom was he speaking at the time? These three points are to be taken into consideration before any conclusion can be drawn around any subject.

I like Swamiji's idea, however, that the "top ten" should stop eating meat, i.e., royalty, the rich, etc., for they do not labor physically, so they do not need to eat flesh. And for those who have cultivated yogic abilities, they too can eat sparsely and lightly, giving up harming animals in accord with observances of nonviolence. The Great Master said that "...*in the Kali Yuga, a man's life depends upon food.*" He is talking about the masses that have to make their living day to day via hard labor.

"I'm enduring my emotions stoically, as you suggested, but there's one emotion that threatens to oversweep my power of endurance, and that is anger. I want control over this emotion because it serves no constructive purpose at all. It is, purely, simply, and in a straight-up manner, a klishta-vritti. How might I apply the teachings of Vedanta to conquer this enemy so that I do not suffer the added misery of anger, so I do not needlessly upset others, and so that my spiritual life is not damaged? I'm looking for wisdom in the application of the principles of Vedanta, here."

Glad that you are continuing to work on the anger issue. Yes, it rises, then it falls. The entire matter is not so much getting rid of it for good, but rather keeping it at a minimum, and using the occasion of its rising to practice balance in the face of it. That will strengthen the muscle of control in us. As far as what causes it to rise, like these difficult life situations, they will always be there in one form or another so we would be wiser to forbear them when they come without giving vent. As you said so nicely, this is Vedanta, not modern therapy. As you are seeing, and expressing, we need beneficial ways of dealing with it, and with these life situations as well. For the latter, I say again, that we need to live consciously so that we nip problems like anger in the bud, taking away its intensity, deflating it. After all, it deflates us after we give vent to it. We can then "return the favor" by deflating it before it rises.

There is one particular story that illustrates Sri Ramakrishna's take on anger. He and Rakhal were in the Master's room, just "hanging out" together as they were wont to do at times – Rakhal being the Master's "spiritual son." They were quite easy with one another. In walks Latu (Swami Adbhutananda), and while he is there, standing before the Master in solemn formality, Sri Ramakrishna suddenly asked Rakhal to get Him some ice water. "Get it yourself," came the response from Rakhal. Upon hearing this, Latu broke into anger and began yelling at Rakhal about speaking to their Master in that disrespectful way. His tirade went on for several minutes, and all the while Thakur and Rakhal were staring at him in amazement. After Latu's burst of anger died away, the Master looked at him and simply said, *"Anger is demonic; never give rise to it."* We can see that, no matter the situation, Sri Ramakrishna advised guarding against this dangerous passion called *krodha*, and did not even agree with the idea of venting it, as they do in modern therapy. It is bad enough that this passion exists inside, ready to insinuate itself on life, but to let it loose so that it can poison the outer atmosphere is even worse.

There is a metaphor I use with regard to defusing anger, and doing so early on, before it rises. At a big lake, a man stands on the shore and throws a big rock into the water. This symbolizes an act of anger. Now, waves rise from that act and move across the lake, diminishing slowly as time passes. On the other side of the lake, a man lies on the banks with his foot dangling in the water. The waves from the rock, by now very tiny, gently brush against his skin; he hardly feels them.

The man who dropped the rock is the one bothered by anger. The man on the far shore is that one who feels anger coming from far off, and does what is necessary to alleviate it before it gets close. The real teaching here is that anger can be foreseen before it even rises, like the waves heading for the man on the far shore. Such a person has "managed" his anger by seeing what causes it, where it rises from, and defusing it before it overtakes the mind and gets expressed. This foreknowledge is rather like placing one's ear on a railroad track in order to determine if a train is coming from far off, or from nearby. With such precognitive wisdom, one can then simply step off the tracks before the train of anger arrives. In dharmic spiritual circles such practices are designated by the word *asamvedana* — nonreceptivity to desire and other impositions. It is far more advanced than anything modern therapy is playing around with, which, to mention one hurdle there, does not even take into account the many lifetimes a person has lived in which to develop these complexes.

Further, as we might meditate on death, using it to assume the egoless and formless condition so as to prepare for it, in the same way one can meditate, carefully, on anger, and on the situations that perk it in us. Looking back on troublesome situations from a next morning's meditation is a decent way of defusing the passions, but better is only lightly assuming their insinuation and defusing them as they — anger, lust, and jealousy — rise again. Seeing beyond them in this way will allow us that "pause that refreshes" the next time they try to take us by surprise.

So, these are some thoughts on the dynamics of practice with regard to the six passions. One might think that this is all a course in "Emotions 101," but so long as complete control and mature detachment are not ours, 100%, so long must we keep vigil, and utilize methods that work to annihilate these usurpers of our unalloyed, uninterrupted, peace and bliss.

"What I don't understand is why, knowing that sense desires cannot be satisfied, I tend to try to find their satisfaction, like the camel and the thorny bush? I suppose this is the trap of maya and worldly life. Will a strong and consistent sadhana ripen the fruit so that I need not worry about these things taking over and ruining the purpose of this life? Please advise."

Basically the real problem is old habit, and that takes a while to break — especially when the entire culture, and most of the world's people, are following the *bhoga marga* — the path of enjoyment. But you are right that some time must be spent in the opposite direction, i.e., sadhana, in order to snap those bonds and get free. One needs a good teacher and an ongoing practice, and you have both of those now. You need only go forward and seek to avoid compromise in the more important endeavors of life. Concerning what Vedanta thinks of as the less important endeavors — daily life, job, finance — you must only model them after spiritual life and subject them to the dharma, as you are beginning to do. Holy Mother loved perseverance most of all, along with patience. These two can move mountains in the interim stages of practice. So patience, perseverance, purity, and practice....and peace. Many functional things come in fives.

"Please elaborate on how assault by the aspirant on the fourth chakra can create a habit of failure in spiritual life? Is it because there is no reason not to gain this level immediately?"

First of all, do not "assault" the fourth chakra, but rather assault the subtle membrane of ignorance (*vishnugranthi*) that envelopes and blocks access to it, to the *Anahata Chakra*. To put it simply, disintegrate the contents of such membranes, like ignorance, fear, and doubt, and then give up brooding on all three. Fix the mind, as the Upanisads advise, only on *"what is Real, what is True, what is Beneficial,"* and *"swiftly reach the Goal of human existence."*

If one does not take immediate action in this matter, and falls into the daze of brooding and indeterminacy, then what Patanjali calls *alabdhabhumikatva* and *anavasthitatvani* take hold. Simply put, this amounts to the "one step forward and two steps back" problem in spiritual practice. The aspirant should avoid this by hearing the Truth, contemplating the Truth, and realizing the Truth when it is presented by the guru via the tradition one selects. People without a guru and a practice will never even come to know of things like chakras, enlightenment, and the subtle knots (granthis) that obscure them. How then can they contemplate and realize them?

Then, and more in the direction of your question, the seeker also has to be careful of repeated failure. That instills the opposite of what is wanted in the mind. A swift and direct access to higher levels of consciousness is most desirable, and there is no reason why, if the teacher is adept, and the sadhika is qualified, that it should not be possible. Of course, in this world, at this particular phase of time, impediments abound.....

"When meditating on the first chakra and its nectar, what do we ask ourselves in order to see their usefulness? For example, how would I discover the usefulness of sexuality?"

Sexuality in this day and age, and always for worldly beings, amounts to satisfaction of pleasure in an atmosphere lacking higher awareness. The brutes express it animalistically. The hedonists want it for express pleasure. The worldly use it to propagate worldly children for purposes of enjoyment and accumulation of wealth. The puritans are averse to it, and shut it out in secrecy in dark rooms. However, dharmic souls wield it as a way of opening an avenue for the descent and birth of illumined souls into this earth. The lovers of God see it as an expression of Siva and Shakti, the union of sacred male and female principles. In the latter two scenarios listed above, it finally gets deified, and finds higher expression. So deify it, do not defile it!

When encountering the presence of sexuality, then, in early spiritual practice, the breaking of old habits and thought patterns around it, both, are needed. The husband must see the Divine Mother in his spouse; the wife, Lord Siva in hers. Thus will divinity attend upon the householder fold and tradition, and return it to the noble institution that it once was when great Rishis were being born on earth by the hundreds!

"Though I have been persevering in my practice, in the past week there has been some low points to my spiritual consciousness due to my lower self worrying about the spiritual health and progress of my companion. But this has not stultified me, or caused me to not remain resolute in returning to the Source in meditation during the day. But what I think about and question is, in that line of the famous 'Song of the Sanyasin,' that reads, '....no man who thinks of woman as his wife can ever perfect be....,' how would a householder interpret this part of the Song?"

Concerning the householder, that line which goes, "...no man who thinks of woman as his wife can ever perfect be," is an easy one — though most householders never quite come upon the solution. As with most things spiritual in nature, it is simple to comprehend, but difficult to place into practice.

Though married, the husband must learn to look upon the wife as Shakti, as Divine Mother. The wife can never really be yours, since nothing in this world can be yours in the personal sense of the term — only in the universal sense.

Everything has come out of you as mental projection. But one cannot possess a projection, like trying to grab beams of light in the air. In the case of the wife, then, she is yours, and you are hers, for as long as you both want it that way. But that mutual sense of belonging should be cherished mainly on the impersonal level rather than just the personal level. Then you can be perfect, she can be perfect, and you both can strive for perfection and help one another do the same.

If she does help you do that, then she is *vidya shakti* and you should celebrate dharmic life with her. If not, she is *avidya shakti*, and you must look elsewhere for a fitting partner. Time will tell, but advance thinking on the subject, and careful observation, may help you determine and clarify the picture in advance. As many a poor fool has found, it is not ideal to wake up to the truth late in the game, after so much karma has been created, and so little energy is left to finally rectify the situation. As Vivekananda, who wrote the line presently under study, has said: *"All expansion is life, all contraction is death. All Love is expansion, all selfishness is contraction."* So scrutinize all happenings from a balanced position of mind — *sthiti-manasana* — then act and adjust accordingly.

Another issue arises here. Why do people in household life overlook the simple solution just explained? It is due to distraction. They allow their daily and worldly life to completely overshadow their ongoing spiritual practice. Talk about your *viveka* (one's discrimination), a very clear line can be drawn between ordinary life and spiritual life. That line can be defined as the presence of sadhana, or not. If sadhana is gone, God may as well be gone, and will disappear behind the scenes. And Brahman is already far enough behind the scenes that we certainly do not need It to move further away. We need It to come closer — ideally, right into our lives. Oil is already hidden deeply in sesame seeds. What we need is a way to bring it out, to invent an ingenious press to extract it. That press for the householder is called *sadhana*, spiritual self-effort, and it needs constant attention.

So just be fair. In the beginning try giving God and sadhana the same amount of attention that you give to satisfying hunger and thirst, or that you give to your wife and children. That will be the definitive measure. For, if the Truth be known, God is the only loved one anyone actually has. God, Brahman, is the Eternal Companion; all others come and go by and through That. As the Taittiriya Upanisad has it, *"Out of fear of Brahman the wind blows, the sun rises, Indra presides, death bows low, and the cosmic sets of fives carry out their respective functions. The individual soul only becomes fearless when it attains firm and peaceful ground in that Supreme Reality. Even a wise man falls victim to fear if he fails to reflect on Brahman."*

"What is the basis of the teaching of Holy Mother where She urges us not to find fault in others, but look at our own faults?"

The basis of that teaching is really twofold. First, comes humility and its acquisition, and how it correlates with compassion for others, for where they are operating at in their minds. We go the opposite direction in spiritual life. Whereas many others might aver that it is wrong to find fault, we would state it is better to inculcate patience and compassion, and give all the benefit of the doubt where possible.

Secondly, the teaching of not finding fault with others has an implication of a cosmic design. It is connected with the insight that the mind is dual by nature, therefore has all imperfections in it. This realization, gotten over time and with practice and close observation of oneself, makes one humble and takes away self-righteousness. How can one point a finger when one knows that the soul on the receiving end of your finger is as impeded by his or her mind as you are. Better to go about and inform people of the imperfections in mind and nature (which came out of mind), and begin to point that finger at the Atman instead. All of this, the implications, and more, come from Her final pregnant statement to us using Her last breath.

Questions, observations and insights regarding the issues of the day or problems in spiritual life may be directed to Nectar's editorial staff at srvinfo@srv.org and will be duly addressed in succeeding issues.

◆ Dr. Alexander Hixon

ESSENCE OF ADVAITA VEDANTA
Exploring Gaudapada's Nondual Philosophy, Part 2

We continue with a series of lectures that Lex Hixon presented in late 1987 and early 1988, in which he explained the basis and deeper teachings found in Gaudapada's famous Karika on the Mandukya Upanisad. This is the second discourse. A transcription of the final talk will appear in the next issue.

The atmosphere that we can participate in here tonight is very rich and very conducive to deeper understanding. What we do on these Tuesday nights takes a great deal of effort on all of our parts, although it is extreme simplicity that we're trying to gain insight into. It takes a great deal of effort and penetration — almost like a diamond drill — to penetrate into the very heart and essence of Reality. We are very grateful to the atmosphere that is provided by Cafh Foundation, not just the space. And we like looking out on New York City — that's why we keep the blinds open.

Acknowledging Reality

Our approach to Reality is one of eyes wide open. Reality has to be experienced on all levels, in all conditions, on all planes of being, in all the forms of thinking, in all the forms of perception, that humanity has at its disposal — or else it wouldn't be Reality. It would be some sort of special dimension of the universe where you could go to some high yogic state and maybe experience some unique bliss that nobody else can experience in other places in the universe. But we are not satisfied with that. We want to make an approach to the very core and heart of Reality which is everywhere available and evident. You could say that electricity is something like that — it's available everywhere. But sometimes in order to generate electricity, some very, very complicated and powerful mechanisms are necessary. And for this, we have in the spiritual world what's called a spiritual lineage. A great sage is like a great dam that can, as it were, generate an immense amount of electricity, and it can be passed down through the generations — as many generations as there are people who are pure transmitters.

Luminaries, Preceptors, and Lineages

The man whose works we're studying, Gaudapada, lived around 500CE. We're receiving this transmission after 1500 years. In my case, I studied this text and was introduced and initiated into this text by Swami Nikhilananda of the Ramakrishna Order. So, Sri Ramakrishna and his wife, Sarada are really the sources that are generating that kind of electricity — that we're experiencing now, here. That enables me to try to transmit that once more into my times, to the people around me. I'm someone who is a student, a transmitter; not a realizer. That's a very distinct difference.

So in that sense, tonight, we're all students together. But I want to be frank about the fact that there's an electricity, a spiritual energy coming through me from a certain spiritual lineage, in this case, that of Sri Ramakrishna and Holy Mother. So we should realize that it's not an intellectual enterprise, or like a college classroom where we're engaged in academic scholarship. This is really some sort of spiritual transmission.

In these meetings I've tried to lay out enough of a general understanding of Gaudapada in order to arrive at tonight, in which we will study the form of meditation or contemplation — the precise form which he recommends. Now, if you haven't been to any of the previous meetings, it really doesn't make any difference. I think it will become evident to you as we discuss what is basically going on here. But for the rest of us it has been very clarifying to go over the particular approach of Gaudapada and it's major points. It's a very radical approach. One simply has to get used to a very fresh approach to something. I feel after twenty years that I'm still getting used to it. I'm still understanding it better, not just intellectually, but I'm still feeling things revealed by it.

So this evening, as every Tuesday evening, we feel we are making a step together in our spiritual life and spiritual practice. Even if you get one single confirmation, one single glimpse of light in this evening, take it back and nurture it for the following week, and you'll find it growing into something powerful and illuminating.

This is the end of book one of the *Gaudapadakarika* — the last ten verses. I'm going to try to give the basic content of these verses, which are describing a form of meditation, and then we're going to try and practice this together. And then possibly we'll have some questions and answers about that process.

The Word, AUM

Since Gaudapada is from a Hindu background, he selects the seed-syllable, Om, which in Sanskrit is spelled A, U, M. It's still pronounced "Om," you don't have to say, "awm" as some people do, but still you'll find it [the spelling] is important for understanding his meditation. These three letters become symbolic of the three basic modes of awareness. The way that Gaudapada sees the situation is that Absolute Consciousness is always the same, always in a steady state as it were — not even a state — always transcendent, and pure and peaceful, and which is the very nature of the universe. Everything you see, no matter how busy and complicated it might look, is Absolute Consciousness. This Absolute Consciousness has three modes of awareness that it operates through. He calls them objective awareness, subjective awareness and pure awareness.

The letters of Om — A, U, and M — you should identify them contemplatively in your mind with the three modes of awareness. A, the first one, this broad opening —"ah" — symbolizes objective awareness. Objective awareness would contain every bit of interpersonal information. You might call it a whole universe — a huge, vast array of interpersonal information being agreed on by conscious beings, and maybe sometimes not being agreed on — being disagreed on. But that also makes it objective in a certain way — you're arguing a point, you're negotiating a point. So a whole universe really consists of that.

You could say, "isn't there some sort of rock bottom in the universe, and aren't we just projecting our various ideas on it?" Well, that is not Gaudapada's understanding. Nor is it really the understanding of modern science. Ultimately, events exist for observers. Different observers in different levels of awareness will observe different events. So, Gaudapada is not denying the fact that this chair exists — I can sit on it, I'm not falling through it. A modern physicist also wouldn't object to the fact that I'm sitting on the chair. But if the modern physicist wanted to describe the core energy of what's appearing as this chair, it would be something very different. Gaudapada never wants to deny our responsibilities or the set-up of our daily lives. He is like a broad physicist who's going into the very nature of reality of itself — not just the nature of matter, which physics goes into — but the nature of reality, the nature of being. He's finding it as this array of three modes of awareness, and one of them is this objective awareness. That's the "Ah" in Om.

The second mode is subjective awareness. There are many, many levels of experiences that living beings are having which are interpretive in nature. They have to do with, let's say, personal memories of events which no longer exist. So there's this whole rage of structures and structurings which Gaudapada identifies as subjective awareness.

The third mode of awareness is something very surprising, and not so well known to our ordinary thinking process. Gaudapada calls this pure awareness. This means a kind of structureless potency, a structureless reservoir of consciousness out of which the other two emerge.

Succintly, then, these are the three modes. What he calls Absolute Consciousness operates in these modes, but is unaffected by them. I was trying to think of an analogy for this. The question is, how does Absolute Consciousness relate to these three modes of experience? I thought, something like the principle of a musical scale. How does the principle of a musical scale relate to all the different ragas or melodies? They are all composed of the musical scale, but the musical scale is something which exists in principle totally untouched, unaffected by all the different melodies and ragas that you could compose. That's just a rough analogy; please take it as that.

Meditation on the Three Modes of Awareness

What Gaudapada wants to do in this meditation is to suggest how we are going to be able to go from the relative modes of experience to the Absolute Reality. So he says:

Taking the seed syllable OM — A, U, M —
identify that with objective, subjective and pure awarenesses.

In other words, identify that with the entire range of conscious information and conscious potential which we think of as the universe. All of it is this OM. And the A is the broad sound, *ah*. The U is a slightly subtler sound, *oo*. The M, pure awareness, is a kind of extended mmm*mmmm*. So, Aauummm... Aauummm....Aauummm......

Now, this is not uttered to create "good vibrations", or call down some aspect of the Diety, or something like that. Gsudapada does not sport a religious approach to this seed syllable, AUM. He's using it as a symbol for meditation.

As one mentally repeats this mantra OM, if we repeat it out loud, it might sound like we are a cult, or a religious group that's trying to invoke something. But this is not Gaudapada's approach. As we've said before, he leaves religion to exist — but he's interested in something more fundamental than religion. If we understand what he's talking about, then whatever our religious commitments are will be enriched and strengthened, purified, clarified. So, he continues:

As one mentally repeats this mantra OM,
the all encompassing silence itself is meditated on
as Absolute Consciousness.

So, the Ommm is, as it were, floating in encompassing silence, just as all of the modes of experiencing, all the perspectives of experiencing, are sort of floating in this spaciousness of Absolute Consciousness. He explains further:

The "A" sound of OM leads the meditator
through the entire universe of objective awareness.

So, each time one says OM, the "A" sound, as it were, is leading one through anything one can think of in the objective, shared world — the Constitution of the United States, the published letters between Freud and Jung, information that radio telescopes are picking up from the outer parts of the galaxy — all of that is objective awareness. It never ends — the three modes of awareness continue to be in play — but you can stop seeking in the objective mode. You're no longer looking for something someplace in the objective mode of awareness that is going to explain everything.

The "U" sound leads the meditator
through all the various realms of subjective awareness.

Here, all of one's past, all of one's speculations about the future, all of the inexpressible, incommunicable feelings of the present moment — all of that is our subjective awareness. And every being has it. There are billions and billions of beings, so there are billions and billions of realms of subjective awareness. All of this one has to move through. One has to be finished with that. One has to say, "Well, that's not where we're going — that's not where Reality lies."

Now, the 'M' sound, which is prolonged — Ommmm — leads the meditator through pure awareness, which Gaudapada characterizes as fundamentally blissful. It's blissful because in pure awareness, structures don't exist. It's a kind of pure potency — out of pure awareness the various structures come into being. There's a kind of bliss in that. It's the realm where the mystics of various religions have found bliss and union and identity and all of that. What Gaudapada is saying is, even here is

> "....spiritual awakening is what the human being is designed for. It's very, very vast. You have to feel when you're doing this meditation that you really have gone through the entire range of possible experience, and in that sense are finished with them."

not the place to look for the nature of Reality. This is also a mode. So the "mmm" should lead you through all of that, so you're no longer even going to be looking in the realms of bliss, or escape, or release, or liberation, or anything like that.

Thus one is led contemplatively through the whole range of possible experience.

People say, well, you need hundreds and thousands of lifetimes before you can become enlightened, or something like that. Well in this OM there will be hundreds of thousands of lifetimes, because you're going to be led through all of the possible realms of experience. There will be nothing else to experience. Even if you were born as a god in some heavenly realm, or if you're born in some advanced future civilization, you're always going to be within these three modes of relative experience. This allows one to come to an end of all that, not to deny it or cancel it out — it's always in play, and it's real, too. It's not just some sort of illusion. The earth is not an illusion, and heaven is not an illusion, and hell is not an illusion. They're all perspectives. But if we want to get to the root of the whole thing, the root of all reality, we have to follow something like this process that is being suggested.

...and is free therefore to awaken from the three modes of awareness, into, or as, Absolute Consciousness Itself.

Awaken from the Waking State!

The word "awaken" is very important in Gaudapada's philosophy. He feels this is the best way of understanding it — like waking up from a dream. But in this case one is waking up from dreaming, waking, and deep sleep. One is waking up from relative experience as Absolute Consciousness. Awakening is an instantaneous thing. That's why, when we do this meditation, we don't usually spend a long time meditating, because it's an instantaneous insight.

Now, in the Tibetan Book of the Dead, recognizing the Clear Light, as they put it, is like trying to roll a needle sideways down a thread. It might roll one or two revolutions and then it is going to fall off. That's what happens to us when we meditate in this unique fashion. For a second, we may be able to sustain it, then we fall off. But undoubtedly the sages are always in that state, no matter what they're doing at the same time — reading, walking in the street, helping people, or whatever. But they are always in that awakened state of Absolute Consciousness.

We haven't begun to walk this tightrope, but on the other hand I'm convinced that we can all get a glimpse of it. That's why we're gathered here. It would be a waste of time for us to be here if we were just going to read about this wonderful tightrope walker who can do this amazing thing and we can't even begin to do it. We have to be able to get a glimpse of this.

And I'm convinced we can, because the human being is actually designed for this. This spiritual awakening is what the human being is designed for. It's very, very vast. You have to feel when you're doing this meditation that you really have gone through the entire range of possible experience, and in that sense are finished with them. They still continue to flow, but you've graduated them. And it's not a matter of pride, because there's no "you" left. The ego, the "I", is part of all that relative experience you are done with. So there's no patting "yourself" on the back in this graduation. There's no danger of that kind of spiritual pride.

Gaudapada next points out that there is no way to move toward Absolute Consciousness with any contemplative experience or methods of contemplation. He pulls the rug out from under what he's suggesting us to do. Because he says:

We are never actually separate from Absolute Consciousness, which neither comes nor goes.

So there's a paradox here of trying to "push through the final barrier." We are finished with all relative experiences and we're trying to push through this final barrier to get to That. But he is also pointing out that this is a wrong conception. That kind of ambitious pushing through and practicing to get somewhere else means one is still involved in relative experience. He goes on:

All contemplative practices....

— this includes the Jesus Prayer, the *Om Mani Padme Hum*, the keeping of the Sabbath, and art, looking at beautiful sunsets, loving each other, sacrificing ourselves for each other or for our country — all of this is carried on within the three modes of awareness. Whereas —

Absolute Consciousness is utterly unaffected by these three modes, although appearing through them as our experience.
The three modes of awareness have never substantially come into being. There is simply Absolute Consciousness.

This is his ultimate point. I will try to give an analogy, but it's very hard, of this idea of *"never having substantially come into being."* It's like perspectives in a room. You're looking out on Broadway right now. I'm looking at you and seeing this peaceful room of sitting people. These are both legitimate perspectives; they really reflect something. But they have never substantially come into being; there is not a being, a sort of entity, which is looking out on Broadway, nor an entity which is looking toward a group of people. Perspectives change constantly, and if you move around the room you will get countless different perspectives. So the universe is this way. There are countless different perspectives, but there's this one Space, this one Spaciousness in which all of these perspectives are appearing. They never substantially come into being. They haven't existed — they only possess a mode of existence which is relative experience.

So there's nothing to clear away. We don't have to hammer through a wall. We don't have to suppress all sorts of negative feelings. We don't have to do anything in order to awaken as Absolute Consciousness.

Yet we have all sorts of responsibilities: if we get overweight, we should diet. If someone needs a place to sleep, we should try to work out a situation where the homeless can sleep. All of these things continue to carry on. But from the radical standpoint of Gaudapada, all that exists is Absolute Consciousness — in play as Its modes, But Its modes never substantially come into being.

Inspirational Emptiness

Now people might say, well, isn't this depressing? Doesn't this remove our fun in life, or remove one's sense of value in life? No, quite the opposite. It seems to have a tremendously freeing effect on a person, a tremendously strengthening, healing effect, and it seems to generate a tremendous amount of compassion and love as well. It's as if one is finally free to really love the entire Reality, and to be deeply involved in the whole Reality, and not to be burned out by one little corner of it. That's the value of the meditation we're attempting to do.

After we utter this OM together, and once we've identified the 'A', 'U,' and 'M' — deeply, and not just mentally — with the entire range of possible experience, then he states:

> *Simply drop the process of contemplation and awaken,*
> *suddenly, from all experience, as Consciousness Itself.*

Obviously the process of contemplation has to go too. And the great sages and mystics of all the traditions have their way of saying this. It's a very mature thing, and sometimes they only say it to advanced students. But I think all of us are courageous and strong enough to hear this — that all of our efforts and process has to be dropped, that there has to be this sudden awakening.

The Limitations of Individual Experience

Awakening is not an experience. Any experience, no matter how refined or subtle, even an experience of pure bliss without any structures, is all in the mode of relative experience. And that includes the subtle duality of experiencer and what is experienced. Later, Gaudapada will say that the fundamental lack of this realization causes anxiety. Whenever there is a duality, whenever there is this dual structure of experiencer and what is experienced, no matter how comfortable it is, or how beautiful your experience is, there's some sort of subtle anxiety, which is generated by this gap.

And so, this awakening does not come in the form of another experience. Experiences can point to it. Sometimes we've sat and performed some meditation together on these Tuesday evenings, and people have been having imagery in their meditation, and they've shared some of it. And I've tried to indicate where I thought it was pointing to a non-dual, unitive vision, when it was an imagery that was suggestive. But Gaudapada uses this seed syllable OM in order to lead and suggest and point in a certain direction.

One might cease in one's meditation, as it were, just drop it and awaken from experiences. The range of experience still is not canceled out; it's not destroyed. You're not dropping an atom bomb on all of manifest being. So you might see anything. You might see 72nd St., or you might see Buddha or Jesus standing in front of you, you might see a page of the Torah descending in golden letters from the sky. You might just see the ordinariness of everything — it could come in many different ways. But the very important thing is not to identify It with any of those experiences, because we're awakening out of experience.

From this wakefulness — judging from the lives of sages and things they've said, and glimpses that all of us have had — from this position of wakefulness, all experience becomes much more rich, much more delightful, and also much more painful. You look at someone suffering and you don't make it abstract; you feel it more directly. Your life is full of more pain, more joy, etc., so this isn't a kind of lobatomizing of experience; it's an intensifying. In fact, experience will become as intense as we can bear it, and then at a certain point, when we can't bear it anymore, we cancel it out.

Again, you might see anything — you might see Buddha, Jesus, standing in front of you, but we don't identify the non-dual awakening with any of the forms that might appear, or the formlessness that might appear either. It's something that is delightfully and amazingly free and untouched by experience. This is why Gaudapada indicates that this sudden awakening has to be an awakening out of all experience. And he points out that the realm of experience still remains, just as one can realize one is dreaming, without denying the dream. There's no denial of all of the subtle responsibilities and subtle forms of coherence that exist in the realm of objective and subjective awareness. In fact, I feel that a person could become a better mathematician, a better statesman, a more responsible person in the relative structures by having awakened out of the relative structures and being grounded in the Absolute Wakefulness of Consciousness. This is where Gaudapada says,

> *This Absolute Consciousness,*
> *which Upanisadic sages call Brahman.*
> *is free from the subtle anxiety that is always felt*
> *by any separate experiencer.*

This is like having a sort of subtle low-grade fever of anxiety all the time. And it's not a personal anxiety, and it's not paranoia; it's a kind of metaphysical anxiety, a kind of sense of the fundamental gap between one's relative experience and the Truth. This becomes gradually more painful and more visible to people, and that's why all of you are here. I'm absolutely sure there is no one here who is not here because of that gap, because that gap has become, if not painful, at least very evident. In some of your cases, you have had insights in which that gap has been overcome for a second. That, of course, is the positive kind of motivation for being here — one has glimpses of this and obviously wants to extend those glimpses.

The Silence of a Mahamuni

Gaudapada uses the term, *mahamuni*, for the great sage. That's the term in sanskrit, and it's also the term for a Buddha. Muni means silence. There is something essentially silent about the great sage who has awakened as Absolute Consciousness. It's not a silence of necessarily being taciturn, or not being able to think of anything to say, or anything like that. It's a kind of metaphysical silence. As Gaudapada points out, this is because Absolute Consciousness cannot be described. Nothing relative, like an experience, could possibly open up to It. Therefore, the silence of the great sage has something to do with the nature of Absolute Consciousness. The great sage might be someone who wrote poetry, and loved to talk on the telephone. So the silence doesn't have to come in some sort of obvious psychological form; it's a quality of being of the sage. It's the essence, you might say, of the sage. That is why being in the presence of a sage creates a tremendous sense of peace, a tremendous sense of completion and clarity. Then when one walks away, one walks back into one's own identification with relative experience. Then, all one's problems return again. But at least in being in the presence of the sage, something of that silence, which is the essence of this awakening, is communicated. Thus, Gaudapada says:

> *Therefore, the Mahamuni is always spontaneously revered and cherished by all beings.*

This a very lovely concept, and it's because all conscious beings are expressions of Ultimate Consciousness, and therefore in one degree or another, can recognize the great sage. Really, they are recognizing their own root and ground there, somehow being manifested through his or her presence.

Coming to the end of this section, Gaudapada points out that the Upanisads teach two levels of being: manifest being and the Ground of Being, which they call the Higher Brahman and the Lower Brahman. It is just a way of speaking for the instruction of beginners. Speaking from the knowledge of Ultimate Truth, there is nothing that transforms itself into lower or higher. So finally, before we begin our exercise,

> *The three component sounds of OM*
> *may be contemplated as the origin from A,*
> *the manifestation through U, and the dissolution into M,*
> *of all the structures of awareness.*
> *When this cycle has been fully experienced....*

Please place emphasis on the word "fully." You must feel that you've gone through every possibility. You're not going to need one more lifetime, or a million more lifetimes — they would not be able to get you any further through this. When this cycle has been fully experienced through deep contemplation, one is then free to awaken instantaneously as the Absolute Consciousness which both constitutes and transcends the entire play of awareness. Gaudapada goes on to say —

> *This OM is what religious thinkers refer to as the Supreme Lord abiding in the hearts of all beings.*

The Supreme Lord, in this sense, you might say is the Supreme Perspective. Then we have to awaken from that perspective too. And then the Gordian knot has been cut, as it were.

A Short Meditation

As overwhelming as it may seem, we should practice this meditation together now, for a few minutes. Let's begin. We automatically uncross our legs and sit straight — that's a natural position, but remind yourself that you don't have to do anything. We're trying to undo things, not do more things. We're trying to do less things — in fact radically less things. Again, the main thing to use is this seed syllable, OM, but silently, so it doesn't seem like we're invoking some sort of religious ceremony. This is not that, this is pure contemplation of a non-dual nature, which is neither religious nor non-religious.

Auummmm — Let's just get lost in that; that's pure awareness. But have the clear perception that it is also not the Ultimate Reality. Now we are becoming aware of other sounds as we concentrate. Just know, that all the sounds you hear on the street are part of the "A" sound. All the thoughts you're having about your past, your present, or your future, that's the "U" sound. If you're feeling a little bit of bliss, a little bit of release, that's the "M" sound. Now awaken from all of these. Let them be; don't try to police the universe. You can't eliminate the "A", the "U", the "M". They're always there. Awaken, awaken....

Yet, something is telling me that "awaken" is not the right word. You're already awake. We are always awake as Absolute Consciousness. So the effort, if you can call it "effort", is to realize we are ever awake. Now repeat Auummm a few times. Try to sense that if we were to continue this for one more minute, or for another hour, or for ten hours, it would be the same. Sense that.

From Meditation to Appreciation

And that's the meditation. It's a deep meditation because you can't come out of it if you're really serious about it. It stays there, it is a permanent gift and the *mahamuni*, or great sage — he gives that gift. And Gaudapada was kind enough to write the gift down in his Karika. Shankara was kind enough to make commentary on those Karikas, which inspired all the lovers of Shankara in India to preserve this ancient document for 1500 years. If you've ever been to India, you wonder how you can preserve a manuscript for 1500 years — it's pretty amazing. It's hard to preserve anything for fifteen minutes or fifteen years, what to speak of that long a time.

And there is also Sri Ramana Maharshi, who passed in 1951, who fully embodied this stateless State. There are some of the Shankaracharyas in India today who fully embody it. There are Zen masters who embody it, there are Jewish, Christian, and Muslim saints that embody it; so it's not in any danger of disappearing from the earth.

So I would suggest that you take this gift of Gaudapada, which is in the form of the OM, which is a compact symbol for our entire being. Take it with you and use this meditation.

Now we can take some open comments and questions, just swift one liners that may clarify anything that may need clarifying. If you have a shadow of a doubt about how this meditation works, ask me, as it will be a benefit for other people.

Q: Is this different from any mantra or religious practice that we may already have?

A: This does not interrupt that. This is not meant to take us away from that, or denigrate that in any way. So if one is making the Jesus Prayer, or if one is permutating the Hebrew letters in order to have meditative experiences, whatever you're doing in your spiritual life, please continue. This is something which probably is considered in stray moments. Also you could consider it while you're doing your other religious practices if you want to. It shouldn't introduce any sort of confusion, any more than like it shouldn't interfere with one's love life. If a partner in love is embracing you, you can't say, "I'm sorry, I'm really not in the mood, because I'm thinking of this OM and I'm awakening beyond all levels of experience." Don't let it interrupt anything. Live life in all fullness whatever your station of life is. If you're a brahmachari, then you won't have that particular problem. In fact, if you really took it in as we did, (miraculously enough here, in the late 20th century, we really took this in) I don't see how it's going to be possible to forget it. I think you might even wake up in the middle of the night chanting, "OM." Or you might be sitting down to a meal, and it will suddenly come to you. But just as one's spiritual practice does too. Or just one's love for one's loved ones, or one's concern for the world, all of these things, all of these rich feelings arise in one. That's what constitutes one's spirituality. So please know, it's not going to interrupt anything.

(Answering another question:) When you're "going into a blissful place where you don't want to come out," that's a very good expression of pure awareness. That's what Gaudapada means by pure awareness. To go into pure awareness has some renewing or restoring value, and for some people it can be a gate to the non-dual understanding. In other meditations, the goal is to go into pure awareness, and to sort of bask in it. But that's not Gauadapada's approach at all. That's more like a yogic or a mystic type of approach. Gaudapada is not yogic or mystic. He's the path of insight. So in your case, when you're doing this kind of non-dual meditation, you should go back and forth between open eyes and closed eyes. When you close your eyes and begin to go into this pure awareness, feeling deep and profound and blissful, then open your eyes again, and focus back on all the responsibilities of the world, the suffering of the world. Go back and forth and try to equalize them in your mind, because they're just "A", "U", and "M" — they're just these three components. Reality is untouched by all those three.

Now as far as the "power of the OM," it definitely has immense power as a seed syllable in certain mantras in Hinduism and Buddhism, but unless one has received initiation, I don't think the power is too dangerous or too heavy. I think anyone can say OM. They might have subjective imaginations of things that are happening, but I don't think there's any particular danger in saying OM, any more than there's danger in saying "God". Many bad or good things could be done in the name of God, so many bad or good things could be done in the name of OM also.

As Gaudapada says, "*This OM is what religious thinkers think of as the Supreme Lord abiding in the heart of all beings.*" This is what I call the Supreme Perspective in relative existence: this OM, or let's say, "God" in another tradition. But you might ask, "But what about the OM here — you say it's a symbol but doesn't it also have some sort of power?" I think the power that we all experienced during the meditation, if you want to call it "power," or "peace," is part of the real spiritual transmission of Gaudapada and the sages that have practiced this and still practice it in the world today. I think that to some extent, one is tuning into the presence of the great sage, the mahamuni, when one says OM with this kind of instruction, doing this kind of thing. So I would say, definitely, it's not just a symbol, in the sense of,

"Well let's take a symbol of a three-pronged pitch-fork, with one prong for each of the three modes of awareness." I don't think you would get anywhere by meditating on a pitch-fork. I think the OM that's being transmitted here has a kind of illuminating power. But not in the same sense of when it's in a mantra or a religious setting.

(Answering another question:) Don't let the non-dual vision interrupt your devotion. Let's say you're keeping the Shabbas and on Friday night you can feel the Shabbas coming in and you're welcoming the Shabbas Queen. You don't have to say, "Oh, it's all the same, this is an illusion; Friday night is the same as any other night of the week." It's not! Because part of subjective awareness is not just scientific data, it's religious data also. I would say, keep your beautiful devotional temperament, your access to subjective awareness, and to pure awareness, but then throw this in as a pinch of spice.

The laughter and the humor around it is so important because around the sage Sri Ramakrishna, for instance, people were really cracking up and laughing most of the time. It shows a great healthiness. Heavily religious people, or heavily political people (people who are heavily into some kind of relative experience) are not humorous, they're not light, they're not relaxed. So in a certain sense, this non-dual taste, this pinch of spice, begins to have a wonderful effect on one's life, and on the life of the whole society.

> The OM as Absolute Consciousness Itself
> is not related to the countless mantras or religious symbols.
> Yet, this OM contains all such mantras and symbols.
> To realize Absolute Consciousness through the OM
> is to be fundamentally free from the dualistic pattern
> of experiencer and what is experienced.
> The sage who knows in this way the OM,
> as well as all other religious symbols and methods,
> is the muni, or silent one, who's speaking and thinking
> are essentially at peace as Absolute Consciousness.

Lex Hixon received his Ph.D. in World Religions from Columbia University in 1976. From about 1971 to the late 80's he conducted a weekly radio show in New York City called "In The Spirit," (ITS) interviewing spiritual teachers from around the world. In the years that followed he entered into deep, serious study and practice of several of the world's religious traditions, eventually becoming a masterful teacher in some of them — including the western chapter of the Jerrahi Order of Istanbul with its several tekkas. Among his books are *Great Swan, Mother of the Universe, Heart of the Koran, Atom from the Sun of Knowledge, Mother of the Buddhas,* and *Living Buddha Zen.* For more information inquire at: **www.lexhixon.org** For ITS Series information inquire at: **www.srv.org**

◆ *Swami Brahmeshananda*

LADDER OF SPIRITUAL ASCENT IN JAINISM

In the mystic literature of almost all the major religions of the world, the stages through which a spiritual aspirant advances from the lowest to the highest level of spiritual attainment are found described in greater or lesser detail. Apart from their theoretical importance, such descriptions have been of practical value. They help an aspirant to assess his progress, to determine where he stands on the ladder of perfection, to see the next step ahead, and to undertake necessary means to climb on to it. However, the descriptions of spiritual unfolding vary from one religion to another, and even from one luminary to another, since they depend upon the spiritual technique employed. For example, the progress of a spiritual aspirant practising the Yoga of Patanjali is assessed according to the depth of concentration achieved, while the devotional schools determine a soul's progress according to its proximity to the Lord. Jainism lays great stress on moral life and conquest of passions. The progress in this religion, therefore, is determined on the degree of moral perfection achieved.

According to Jainism, each soul is inherently pure, conscious, blissful, omniscient, and omnipotent, but owing to past karmas, its inherent perfection is concealed. The task before the aspirant is to prevent the accumulation of new karmas (*samvara*) and to remove the already accumulated ones (*nirjara*). To the extent the karmic covering is made thinner, the light of the soul shines forth, just as the sun shines with all its glory the moment fog is removed. Since karmas are also responsible for moral imperfections, spiritual progress is determined by the extent of the removal of karmic impurities. A brief account of the karmas as described in Jainism is therefore imperative in this context.

Karmas According to Jainism

Karmas are classified into eight main types, four of which are *ghatin*, or obscuring, and four *aghatin* or non-obscuring. The four ghatin karmas are *jnanavaraniya*, *darsanavaraniya*, *mohaniya* and *antaraya*; they obstruct the soul's infinite knowledge, faith, bliss, and power respectively. The four aghatin karmas are *ayus*, *nama*, *gota* and *viddanta*; they determine the soul's longevity (period of embodiment), personality, species, and the experience of pleasure and pain in a given span of life. They, however, do not obstruct the soul's perfection. From the point of view of spiritual ascent, mohaniya karmas are the most important. These are twenty-eight in number and are classified into two main categories titled *darsana mohaniya* and *caritra mohaniya*. The darsana mohaniya, three in number, obstruct the faith and right attitude of the soul and are responsible for keeping it at the three lowest rungs of the spiritual ladder. The twenty-five caritra mohaniya karmas prevent the soul from following right conduct and are responsible for desires and passions, and for various grades of immoral conduct. These are of two types: those responsible for sixteen *kasayas* and those responsible for nine *no-kasayas*. There are four basic kasayas or evil tendencies or passions: anger, egoism, deceit, and greed or attainment (*krodha, mana, maya, lobha*). Each of these has four degrees.
1. *anantanubandhin* — intense deep rooted and permanent
2. *apratyakhyani* — involuntary and uncontrollable
3. *pratyakhyani* — voluntary and controllable
4. *samjvalanas* — mild, in seed form only

When a person neither considers anger and other passions as evil, nor abstains from acts prompted by them, he is said to have anantanubandhi karma, since it would entail ananta, or infinite bondage. Next, although one may not justify one's evil tendencies, when owing to long-standing habit they become instinctive and uncontrolled, they are said to belong to the second degree known as apratakhyani. When, however, one is able to control them at will, they are called pratyakhyani. Finally, when these passions persist only in their seed form, without external manifestation, they are called samjvalana. The task before the aspirant is to overcome these passions by degrees.

There are nine *no-kasayas*, the quasi-passions, which can stimulate the production of kasayas, or passions. These include three types of sex desires (called veda) and laughter, attachment, aversion, fear, sorrow, and hatred (*hasya, rati, arati, bhaya, soka, and ghrna*). These are eliminated only in the ninth and tenth stages, when most of the kasayas are removed. The progress of the soul from the fourth to the twelfth step in spiritual development is determined by the elimination of caritra mohaniya karmas. In the thirteenth stage, the remaining three ghatin karmas are eliminated. Finally, the soul ascends to the fourteenth and final stage and attains total freedom when the aghatin karmas too are removed.

Jain scholars recognize two paths by which spiritual ascent can take place: (a) by destruction (*ksaya*) and (b) by suppression (*upasama*) of the karmas. These paths are called *ksapaka sreni* and *upasama sreni* respectively. The difference between them become evident in the first four stages, and in stages from the seventh to the eleventh. An aspirant traveling by upasama sreni sooner or later slips down to the lower stages.

It may be pointed out here that there are two views regarding the importance of external renunciation and conduct. According to one view, internal renunciation, purity of intention, nobility of character, and knowledge are all important, irrespective of purity of action and flawlessness of conduct. One may commit the vilest crime, yet remain completely free from sin if one is totally unattached. On the same grounds, even though a householder may not be able to practise moral virtues to the highest perfection, he can still attain liberation. The other view, also held by Jainism, holds that although intention is important, action too is equally important, and perfection cannot be

> *"Mithyatva,* a state of ignorance of or perverted attitude towards one's real nature, duty, and aim of life, is described in detail in Jain literature. This is the lowest rung of the ladder, and a person standing here cannot even be considered a Jain...."

achieved unless both are perfected. Hence a monk alone can attain the higher perfection, although in exceptional cases a householder may also reach the goal. Even in such cases, the conduct of the person must be immaculate irrespective of whether he takes monastic vows or not.

Among those who lay equal stress on both external and internal renunciation, some are of the opinion that external renunciation must be the result of internal renunciation or should follow it. Others hold that one may initially renounce externally and perfect one's conduct even before inner perfection is achieved, as an aid and a preliminary step to the latter. It can be safely assumed that Jainism holds the second view.

Another subject intimately related to spiritual ascent is that of *dhyana*, or meditation. In Jainism all thinking, or dhyana, is classified into four types: *arta* or sorrowful, *raudra* or violent, *dharma* or virtuous and *sukla* or pure. Of these, the first and the second spring from anxiety, anger, violent desires, and craving for senses pleasures, and are spiritually degrading. The third consists of purification by religious thoughts. The fourth is pure concentrated meditation undertaken in very high stages of spiritual development. Each of these four dhyanas has four sub-types.

With these preliminary remarks, let us now study serially the various steps of spiritual ascent called *gunasthanas* in Jainism. For additional clarity, a chart on page 19 is included.

1st Stage: Mithyatva Gunasthana

Mithyatva, a state of ignorance of or perverted attitude towards one's real nature, duty, and aim of life, is described in detail in Jain literature. This is the lowest rung of the ladder, and a person standing here cannot even be considered a Jain, since he lacks even a basic understanding of the path. He has erroneous notions about reality and mistakes untruth for truth, adharma for dharma, and vice-versa. He is extrovert, sensuous, and strives for sense-enjoyments, which he considers the goal of life. He has no moral guidelines. Psychologically, he is overpowered by desires and passions, and possesses to an intense degree the passions of anger, greed, egotism, and deceit. Another feature of a person at this stage is bigotry, narrow-mindedness, and obstinacy regarding his erroneous beliefs. He has either no intellectual capacity to reassess his preconceived notions, or lacks the willingness to modify them.

Most worldly people belong to this gunasthana. Some may, in due course, awaken to the right attitude and gradually advance towards perfection. This stage also includes materialists and those who do not accept a spiritual goal of life, though they may be morally more advanced than mere brutes.

Right attitude (*samyag-darsana*), right knowledge (*samyag-jnana*), and right conduct (*samyag-caritra*), are the three pillars of Jainism. In the mithyatva gunasthana, all these three are obstructed. When right attitude and faith awaken, the individual ascends to the fourth gunasthana.

4th Stage: Avirata-Samyag-Drsti Gunasthana

As the name suggests, the individual in this state gains right attitude (*samyag-drsti*) towards reality and about one's own nature and aim of life, but is not able to abstain from undesirable actions (*avirata*). This stage marks the beginning of a righteous life and is given great importance in Jainism. The individual in this stage gives up his obstinacy and corrects his erroneous beliefs and notions. He gains right attitude although he is not able to act accordingly. He has right vision but his conduct is not in accord with his faith. He neither abstains from sense pleasures nor desists from causing injury to creatures.

Samyag-drsti literally means right vision. Its original meaning was right attitude or vision regarding life and about oneself. However, in course of time the meaning changed to "right faith," and thus traditionally samyag-drsti means faith in prophets, saints, scriptures, and the tenets of Jainism, without which none can be a Jain nor ascend to the fourth step of the spiritual ladder. This stage can be compared to "conversion" or spiritual awakening, and is understandably given great importance in Jainism, as in all other religions. Faith, undoubtedly, is the basis of all spiritual endeavor, and the greater the faith, the more the chances of spiritual advancement. Although a man with strong faith runs the risk of becoming bigoted, shallowness of faith makes one unstable and confused.

No one can ascend the fourth gunasthana unless he has suppressed or conquered the darsana mohaniya karma and the anantanubandhin quartet of passions. If these are merely suppressed, the individual remains in danger of slipping back to mithyatva. In other words, if one accepts faith blindly, or for some ulterior motive without being convinced of its significance, it will not remain permanent. If, however, faith is backed by deep conviction and understanding regarding the value of morality, higher life, it will remain stable.

3rd Stage: Samyag-Mithyatva-Drsti Gunasthana

The order of describing the gunasthanas has been deliberately altered here since in spiritual ascent the soul reaches the fourth stage directly from the first and can come to the third and second stages only in descent. Thus, the third and the second are stages of decline and can be experienced only after one has "tasted" the right attitude of the fourth stage.

The third stage is a stage of doubt when an individual vacillates between right and wrong attitudes (*samyag-mithya-drsti*). Truth and falsehood both appear equally valid and the individual is not able to differentiate between them. Nor is he able to decide whether to lead a life of sense-enjoyment or of self-con-

> "Samyag-drsti literally means right vision. Its original meaning was right attitude or vision regarding life and about oneself. However, in course of time the meaning changed to "right faith," and thus traditionally samyag-drsti means faith in prophets, saints, scriptures, and the tenets of Jainism...."

trol and righteousness. According to scholars, this stage of indecision cannot last longer than 48 minutes (*antarmuharta*) when the individual either ascends to the fourth or descends to the second stage.

2nd Stage: Sasvada Gunasthana

This is a momentary stage of transition between the third and first stages when the individual retains the memory of the right attitude experienced in the fourth stage. Individuals in the first and second stages do only the first two types of undesirable thinking. Dharma dhyana is possible only in the third and subsequent higher stages.

5th Stage: Desa-Virata Samyag-Drsti Gunasthana

Although numerically the fifth, from the point of view of spiritual aspiration and struggle, this is the first stage. In this stage an individual becomes an avowed householder, a *sravaka*, by taking the twelve vows of a householder. He gives up prohibited and immoral acts and restricts his sense-gratifications and selfish activities. He now labours to control these aspects of the four kasayas which had become instinctive, and over which he had no control (apratyakhyani).

6th Stage: Pramatta Sarva-Virata Gunasthana

At this stage a Jain becomes a true spiritual aspirant. He ascends to a higher stage of moral development. He now spontaneously desists from those sinful practices which he had earlier tried to bring under voluntary control (pratya-khyani). He takes formal monastic vows and becomes a *sramana*. He is now a *sarva-virata*, one who abstains from all external sense-gratifications and from causing injury to creatures. But he is still pramatta, not sufficiently careful to avoid occasions of sin or sinful thoughts (*pramada*). Owing to attachment to the body and obligation to maintain it, he may commit such acts as may cause harm to other living creatures. Evil tendencies and passions (kasayas) persist in subtle form (*samjvalana*). For example, he may not get outwardly angry but cannot help getting irritated or mentally annoyed. However, a clear concept of the goal and abstinence from evil actions greatly helps him to gain strength for subtler, harder struggles ahead. An aspirant at this stage may engage in activities like preaching and writing etc., for the good of others.

7th Stage: Apramatta Samyag Gunasthana

This stage is reached when an aspirant, now a monk, is able to detach his consciousness, or atman, from the gross physical body temporarily, and to relinquish the idea of agency. He also gains sufficient mental alertness, *apramatta*, to avoid minor defects and lapses caused by carelessness. However, since identification with the gross body is hard to overcome, the aspirant cannot stay longer than 48 minutes in this stage and slips back to the lower one. Most monks live oscillating between these two stages. Ultimately, however, the aspirant is able to totally relinquish body-consciousness and ascend to the eighth stage.

In this gunasthana the aspirant totally gives up all thinking of violence, untruthfulness, theft, and hoarding, which constitute the four types of raudra dhyana. He may still engage in arta dhyana, but most of his time is spent in dharma dhyana and its modifications. He can also do the first type of sukla dhyana.

The journey from the seventh stage onwards proceeds in two ways, depending upon whether the subtle passions (kasayas) are suppressed (upasama sreni) or destroyed (ksapaka sreni). During the initial stages, suppression to some extent is inevitable, but sooner or later the aspirant will have to eradicate the subtle deep-rooted passions. If he proceeds on the moral path by the upasama sreni, he will reach the eleventh stage from where he will fall down to the seventh. But if he roots out the passions, he will ascend to the twelfth stage directly from the tenth, from where there is no fall.

8th Stage: Apurvakarana Gunasthana

This is a special stage, and a very important milestone in the spiritual journey. It is characterized by a unique and hitherto unexperienced (*apurva*) joy, and various spiritual realizations consequent on the reduction of karmic coverings. There is no more identification with the body, and among passions, only subtle greed and deceit (*samjvalana lobha* and *maya*) remain.

Another special feature of this state is the acquisition of sufficient spiritual energy to undertake the subtle intense struggle ahead. The aspirant realizes in retrospect that the soul's journey so far has been made possible not so much by its inherent strength – though it had always tried to manifest its inherent powers – but with the help of favourable circumstances. The journey further on will predominantly be through self-effort rather than through destiny. For the first time the aspirant gets a glimpse of the desired goal and feels certain of its attainability.

The seeker's spiritual strength and mastery over karma manifest themselves at this stage in the form of a five-fold technique called *apurvakarana*, through which the aspirant rapidly reduces his karmas. The technique consists of:

1. *sthitighata* — reducing the duration of fruition of past actions (*karma vipaka*)
2. *rasaghata* – minimizing the intensity of fruition of actions
3. *guna-srenu* — arranging karmas in a way that their effect can be experienced even before the actual time of their fruition;
4. *guna-sankramana* - transforming the nature of the effect of

(continued on page 31)

The Ladder of Spiritual Ascent According to Jainism

NO	Name of Gunasthana	Condition of Bondage	Dhyana	Duration
14	Ayogi-Kevali (Siddha-Videha Mukta)		4	Shortest
13	Sayogi-Kevali (Arhat, Jivanmukta)		3	48 minutes or longer
12	Kshina-Moha (Moral Perfection)		2 SUKLA	48 minutes
11	Upashanta-Moha		1	48 minutes or Less
10	Sukshma Samparaya		DHARMA	48 minutes or Less
9	Anivrttikarana			48 minutes or Less
8	Apurvakarana			48 minutes or Less
7	Apramatta Samyak	SAYOGA		48 minutes
6	Pramatta Sarva-Virata (Monk)		ARDA DYANA	48 minutes to Indefinite
5	Desha-Virata Samyak Drsti (Avowed Householder)	KASAYA		48 minutes to Indefinite
4	Avirata-Samyag-Drsti (Faith)	PRAMADA		48 minutes to Indefinite
3	Mishra Samyak-Mithyatva (Doubt)	AVIRATI		48 minutes
2	Sasvada (Undesirable thinking)	Mithyatva	RAUDRA	Momentary
1	Mithyatva (Ignornce)			Indefinite

Classification of Karmas and Their Relation with Gunasthanas:

- AYUS
- NAMA
- GOTRA
- VEDANA
- ANTARAYA
- DARSANAVARANIYA
- JNAHAVARANIYA
- LOBHA
- REST 6
- VEDA
- MAYA
- MANA
- KRODHA
- PRAMADA
- PRATYAKHYANI
- APRATYAKHYANI
- ANANTANUBANDHIN
- SAMYAKTVA M.
- MISRA M.
- MITYATVA M.

NOKASAYA — KASAYA — CARITRA — MOHANIYA — DARSANA

AGHATIN KARMAS — GHATIN KARMAS

◆ Annapurna Sarada

The Gunas
In Vedic Cosmology and Psychology

The teaching of the three gunas helps the soul think in terms of modes rather than moods so as to transcend limitations by locating the cause of dualities in nature and assigning it there. This article is based on Annapurna Sarada's blog published on Advaita Academy's website, Nov., 2011. *(advaita-academy.org)*

Repetition of the teachings is essential in spiritual life. There is a tendency in our modern culture to think that reading or listening once to a teaching and moving on to the next one constitutes "study" or "gaining knowledge," but for most people, the ability to concentrate is not well-developed. A single pass through a scripture, spiritual book, teaching audio, or even one's teacher's lecture on a particular topic, often does not penetrate the surface due to the presence of the gunas. This is not only an issue in spiritual studies, but also secular. A mind trained in concentration will pierce through resistance *(tamoguna)* and distraction *(rajoguna)*, but for most people, those very conditions will prevent concentration to begin with, and their presence will veil or distort comprehension.

Defining, Recognizing, and Understanding the Gunas

What are the Gunas? When beginning the study of Vedanta it can be hard to get a handle on these three fundamental qualities that the rishis of India perceived with their well-honed and subtle intelligence. They are unique to Vedic cosmology and philosophy. The gunas can be said to be the beginning and end of all objective experience. "Objective" here does not mean "fair" or "even-handed" but quite literally the "experience of objects," whether they are physical or conceptual. Any object requires an observer, thus "objective experience" means we are in the realm of duality: Subject and object, I and other, Witness and that which is witnessed, the Seer and the seen. The gunas are the gateway and material foundation of all phenomena, and are the last barrier to *Kaivalya* (isolation/freedom) from the limits of Nature/phenomena. We are exhorted to become *tri-guna-atita*, beyond the reach of the three gunas.

As a foundational concept in Vedic cosmology, the gunas are essential for our understanding of Vedanta, Sankhya, Yoga, and Tantra. This is not only a matter of gathering facts pertinent to a philosophical system; recognition of the gunas is a rudimentary and efficient way to identify the changing and the Unchanging, and practice discrimination between them in order to gain peace of mind. The many and varied ways that discrimination or analysis is put forward throughout the teachings also have the thread of the gunas running through them, whether overtly stated or not.

The gunas – sattva, rajas, and tamas – are the warp and woof of our experience as embodied beings. They are the constituents of *Prakriti*, Nature in its manifest or unmanifest states. This point is important. Prakriti, Nature, is used here in a cosmological sense, as a principle rather than in its association as beautiful vistas, oceans, trees, creatures, etc. Nature as a cosmic principle is insentient and is the material substance of phenomena, and since Vedic cosmology is concerned not just with gross or tangible/atomic matter, this means Nature also includes subtle and causal phenomena, each more "fine" than the last. Prakriti/Nature includes the "Big Bang" but particularly the subtle (ideational) and causal (seed) processes and phenomena that precede the gross manifestation. Thus, most of Nature is unmanifest, that is, it is formless but has infinite potential for form, just like a bell has infinite sound waves potential within it, or a pomegranate has infinite trees potential within it.

Simply stated, rajas is energy, tamas is inertia, and sattva is balance [see chart, "The Twenty-Four Cosmic Principles" on facing page]. These three are in equilibrium when Prakriti is unmanifested *(avyaktam* or *pralaya)*, a formless state in which all worlds/dimensions, objects, and beings are in potential, i.e. formless. When the gunas go out of equilibrium, then, like the striking of a great cosmic bell, all the worlds, objects, and beings come rushing into manifestation, from subtle/conceptual to gross/physical, which, from the standpoint of limited human awareness, appears to take billions of years – and that is only for the atomic/physical part; the subtle realms, corresponding to heavens of various kinds, precede the atomic structures of the physical realm. However, from the standpoint of the stationary cosmic Witness (the Sentient principle), it is only like passing from the formless potential of deep sleep (the "void" since it is void of form), to dream, and then to wakefulness – and with the ability to reverse the process too. According to the Vedic view, this goes on in never ending cycles, and the question of a "first cycle" is a non sequitur. One can thus see how the gunas are that crucial gateway between the realms of phenomena and what lies beyond even the potential for phenomena. That is, one must transcend even the gunas in equilibrium to realize oneself as That which is ever free and never bound by time, space, causation, name, or form.

Phases of Time and States of Awareness

As in the cosmos, so in the individual – this is a truism of Vedic cosmology and psychology. The cosmic pralaya at the end and beginning of a cycle of manifestation is essentially nondifferent from the deep sleep of the individual, wherein the sleeper experiences a lack of form, i.e. no objects, no thoughts, not even an ego. The gunas in one's deep sleep state are also in equilibrium. There is absence of form, but not absence of potential for

The Twenty-Four Cosmic Principles of Samkhya Philosophy

"There are two eternally-existing principles...." Lord Kapila

A) Purusha — Sentient Soul, The Self
(Conscious Spiritual Entity; Ishvara; Brahma-Vishnu-Shiva)

B) Prakriti — Insentient Nature, the Nonself
(Unconscious Material-energy; Unmanifested Nature; Intangible Matter)

** Prakriti consists of Three Gunas in Equilibrium:
- Sattva: luminosity, purity, buoyancy, harmony — it produces pleasure/happiness
- Rajas: activity, energy, movement — it produces pain
- Tamas: dullness, inertia, darkness, stasis — it produces stupor

"Like a magnet, Prakriti attaches itself to Purusha and receives Its conscious rays." Kapila

---

1. Mahat — Cosmic Mind
(Initial disequilibrium, most subtle, most sattvic, most pure)

"The Mahat is a vehicle for the Purusha's consciousness, and a medium between soul and nature. A small portion of It becomes the individual buddhi of man." Lord Kapila

The Eight Origins: 1-3, & 15-19

2. Buddhi — Intellect
(Faculty of discrimination, intelligence)

The 16 Evolutes 4-14, & 20-24

3. Ahamkara — Ego
(The "I"-maker, sense of separate self, beginning of name and form)

Sattvic Ahamkara ←→ Rajas ←→ Tamasic Ahamkara

4. Manas — Mind

Jnanendriyas — 5 Cognitive Senses
5. Shravenindriya — Hearing (sound)
6. Sparshendriya — Feeling (touch)
7. Chakshurindriya — Seeing (form)
8. Rasanendriya — Tasting (taste)
9. Ghranendriya — Smelling (smell)

Karmendriyas — 5 Active Senses
10. Vagendriya — Speaking (speaking)
11. Hastendriya — Handling (acting)
12. Padendriya — Locomotion (moving)
13. Upasthendriya — Procreating (sexual)
14. Payuindriya — Excreting (eliminating)

Tanmatras — 5 Subtle Elements
15. Shabda — Audibility
16. Sparsha — Tangibility
17. Rupa — Visibility
18. Rasa — Flavor
19. Gandha — Odor

Panchamahabhutas — 5 Elements
20. Vyoma — Ether
21. Marut — Air
22. Teja — Fire
23. Ap — Water
24. Ksiti — Earth

Chart by Babaji Bob Kindler
Property of SRV Associations

"The twenty-three evolutes are the non-self; the Purusha alone is the Self. This realization eradicates pain permanently and totally." Lord Kapila

then we enter the waking state. This cycle continues interminably throughout an individual lifetime. The ability to arrest the shiftings of the gunas in the mind affords one the ability to meditate and enter the lower (seeded) samadhis (*savikalpa/samprajnata*) at will. Transcending the gunas entirely, one goes beyond unmanifested Prakriti, to Brahman, also described as going beyond the barrier of unknowing in deep sleep, to the all-pervasive Awareness called *Turiya*, and attains Liberation.

Sankhya and the Gunas

From the very basic definition of the gunas given above, more specific descriptions for each of the gunas are used, depending upon whether one is analyzing just the cosmological ramifications of the gunas or the psychological. Sankhya philosophy organized Vedic cosmology into the 24 Cosmic Principles, and most Indian philosophical systems have used it for its foundation. With regard to evolution, as we have seen, rajas is defined as activity, a force of impetus. Tamas refers to the tendency toward inertia, which leads to stability and solidity. Hence, the subtle elements (*tanmatras*) and the gross elements (*pancha mahabhutas*: space, air, fire, water, earth), all have a predominance of tamas in them. Earth (the principle of solidity, not just soil) is the grossest/densest principle – the furthest evolution of tamas – giving stability to all solid objects in the universe of our waking state. Rajas provides the stimulus for the combining and recombining of the subtle elements that moves evolution from subtle/ideational/conceptual to gross states.

Sattva is the tendency toward balance and the medium through which the Light of Consciousness gets manifested. For instance, the most sattvic principle in manifestation is *Mahat*, the Cosmic Mind, then comes Cosmic and individual Intelligence, Ego/*Ahamkara*, and then individual mind (*manas*). The five senses of knowledge (hearing, touching, seeing, tasting, smelling) evolve out from individual mind. The entire process moves from subtle to gross, or stated in another way, from greater to lesser manifestations/reflectors of Consciousness. All of Prakriti is insentient. However, the Sentiency of *Purusha*, the Self, gets expressed via those principles that partake more of the sattva guna. Those principles evolving out of tamas and rajas comprise the objective world – the objects of mind and senses. This is a basic rendering from the Sankhya view.

Vedanta and the Gunas

For the psychological applications, we can turn to Shankaracharya, among others. Understanding the gunas from this perspective guides our spiritual practice, leads to detachment from the fluctuations of the mind, and ultimately to control of the mind. In his *Vivekachudamani*, Shankara fleshes out the three gunas by explaining that tamas is the concealing power (*avarana shakti*) that hides the nature of Reality, the nondual, all-pervasive, Self-aware Consciousness designated as *Nirguna Brahman* (*nir*, without gunas). Shankara defines rajas as the projecting or "de-centralizing" power (*vikshepa shakti*) that brings forth multitudinous forms. Sattva, then, is the revealing power that penetrates through the darkness of tamas and the myriad projected forms of rajas.

Below are placed excerpts of Shankara's description of the Gunas, (Swami Turiyananda, translation, Sri Ramakrishna Math, Chennai):

"...*The power of decentralizing [projection] is rajas, from which all the desires spring. What are its effects? Constant attachment and all the disturbances of the mind, sorrow, and pain. It is the cause of bondage. The properties of rajas are desire for enjoyment, anger (from obstruction to enjoyment), greed, pride, envy, egotism, and jealousy.*" (vs. 111-12)

In common terms, a person under the influence of rajas is distracted by countless things: objects of need or want, relationships, social and global events, state of health, of livelihood – and all of these in terms of positioning oneself to get what is pleasurable and avoid what is painful.

"*The property of tamas is to cover.... It makes things appear to be what they are not, and that is the cause of bondage [transmigration in ignorance], and even of decentralization [projection]. ...What a tremendous power this tamas has! Even he who has knowledge of the Atman, who is versed in the scriptures, very intelligent, who has very keen insight — even such a person, engrossed in tamas — cannot understand the Atman, even when explained in many different ways; but he takes the attributes of Maya as the Atman.*" (vs. 113-14)

These attributes of Maya begin with name, form, time, space, and causation (which according to Swami Vivekananda is the definition of Maya). These attributes lead to the six transformations afflicting all embodied beings, known as birth, growth, disease, old age, decay, and death. Since tamas covers the true nature of the Self, then one thinks the body is the Self and takes the experiences of the body-mind complex to be happening to the Self. Tamas manifests psychologically as ignorance, dullness, inadvertence, torpor, delusion, and depression.

"*Sattva is pure. It becomes useful for liberation. Therein is reflected the shadow of the Atman [Self]. Sattva manifests the Atman, as the sun manifests the whole of the universe. It is light....* (vs. 117) *Sattva becomes mixed with rajas and tamas, and the traits of mixed sattva are as follows: ... [absence of pride], denial of things [yamas], observance of the niyamas (purification, austerity, study, contentment, and worship of God), control of the [sense] organs, faith, devotion, desire for liberation, a divine nature, and cessation from things that are not good for self-purification, harmlessness, truthfulness, freedom from greed, continence, and absence of acquisitiveness.*" (vs. 118)

Under the influence of mixed sattva, one intuits that the phenomenal world is not ultimately real and that the experiences of pleasure and pain generated by desire for the world lead only to more of the same. Thus mixed sattva makes possible the ability to practice discrimination between the Self and the non-Self, the Unchanging (what is beyond the gunas) and the changing (the ever shifting gunas). Watching how the gunas shift in predominance, day to day, hour to hour, meditation to meditation, leads to the conviction that the Seer of this activity is changeless and unaffected.

"Pure sattva is blissfulness, realization of the Self, supreme peace of attainment, cheerfulness, and an abiding quality in the Self, by which one becomes ever-blissful." (vs. 119)

One of the purposes in drawing a distinction between the gunas from the perspectives of Vedic cosmology and psychology is to gain a more comprehensive understanding that eventually reveals the inherent connection between the individual mind and the cosmic mind. According to the *Pancadasi*, the difference between the cosmic experience and the individual experience is due to which of the gunas Consciousness is reflecting. The cosmic experience is characterized by pure sattva and is known as *Ishvara*, the Cosmic Being (*Saguna Brahman*, Personal God) who controls Maya. The individual experience is characterized by mixed sattva, rajas and tamas, and is known as the *Jiva*, who is bound by *Avidya* (Ignorance). The Jiva bound by ignorance mistakes the body, mind, and ego as the true Self, takes phenomena to be ultimately real, and thereby relegates, so to speak, its inherently ever free, never bound Consciousness to the assumption of apparent limitation – taking the "attributes of Maya as the Atman." *"When the element of sattva is pure, Prakriti is known as Maya; when impure (being mixed up with rajas and tamas) it is called Avidya [ignorance/nescience]. Brahman, reflected in Maya, is known as the omniscient Ishvara [cosmic being], who controls Maya. When reflected in Avidya it is the Jiva [individual being]."* (Pancadasi, 1.16, Swami Swahananda, trans., Ramakrishna Math, Chennai)

Please note that it is only Brahman manifesting in these two modes. [See Nectar #27, "Cosmic & Individual – Two Modes of One Consciousness]

Command of the Vedic Seers

"Arise, awake, and stop not 'til the goal is reached!" is one of the clarion calls of Vedanta. The beginner will hear this and wonder if the first two words are not reversed. Should it not be, *"Awake, arise?"* But the practical teaching is that if one is experiencing the sleep, dullness, and torpor of tamas, then rajas, activity, should be applied. Nothing of a spiritual nature can be done in tamas, so rajas is necessary to "arise." From there one mixes it with sattvic pursuits such as devotion, study, concentration, and meditation – then one is in a position to "awaken."

But waking up is not yet freedom. Even sattva is a gold chain, anchoring one with increasingly subtle degrees of limited pleasure, joy, or bliss in manifested or unmanifested Prakriti: at the physical level with its six transformations of birth, growth, disease, old age, decay, and death; or the subtle and causal levels with experiences of heavenly realms, even of one's own creation, but always short of full immersion in Brahman, wherein lies ultimate Freedom. The *Upanisads* document how the ancient seers finally saw through this last barrier to complete Freedom, the "goal" in the quote above. Yoga describes one of the obstacles to ultimate Freedom/*Moksha*, as the attachment to subtle bliss. But the "problem" of attachment to subtle bliss is far off for most spiritual aspirants, and sattva is to be strived for. It is the plateau from which final liberation can be approached. As Sri Sarada Devi states, *"Peace is the essential thing. You need peace first and foremost."* This peace is relative peace, sattva, and engenders peace of mind.

Returning to the issue of repetition of the teachings, it is obvious how the gunas and the effect they have on the mind establishes the need for hearing the teachings repeatedly. Taking the teachings when the mind is in tamas is as productive as sleeping on a book hoping to absorb something by osmosis. Listening or studying in a rajasic state of mind is like trying to dive for pearls while wearing flotation devices – the restless, distracted, prideful mind cannot dive into the inner meanings presented, and the view of those pearls of wisdom from the surface of the mind is distorted. The rajasic mind will only be "present" for part of the teachings while it thinks about other things, and then passion-based desire for various ends in one's personal life will skew one's understanding. We need to consider this carefully when the tendency to find fault with the teacher and the teachings arises in the imbalanced mind. In sattva, however, the mind becomes concentrated and the light of understanding shines upon the import of the teachings.

Detachment from and Witness of The Gunas

The practice of daily meditation at regular times and ongoing self-enquiry soon reveal to the aspirant how the gunic cycles are affecting one's mind, moods, and understanding. This knowledge leads to detachment from these modes of the mind, strengthens one's Witness consciousness and will, and clarifies it via direct experience of this most essential point about the gunas: they are part of nature. They are present in the mind of all beings and ceaselessly affect the uncontrolled mind in cycles. But they are incapable of affecting the Self since the Self is not in Nature; the Self is merely associating with the various cosmic principles. The one who realizes via spiritual disciplines – spiritually, not just intellectually or intuitively – that the Self/Atman/Purusha is distinct from Prakriti/Nature, becomes free from the effects of the gunas, thus, free from all limitation.

Annapurna Sarada is the presidenst of SRV Associations and an assistant teacher for the sangha and its children. She also writes a blog for Advaita-Academy.org. To read more about SRV's children's classes and retreats, visit the newsletter archive on SRV's website: **www.srv.org**

Wisdom Facets From the Gem of Truth

Sri Ramakrishna

Holy Mother, Sri Sarada Devi

Mahasanatana Dharma

"The Hindu religion alone is the Sanatana Dharma. The various creeds that you hear of nowadays have come into existence by the will of God and will disappear again through His will. They will not last forever. Therefore I say, 'I bow down at the feet of even the modern devotees.' The Hindu religion has always existed, and will always exist."

(Gospel of Sri Ramakrishna)

The Absence of Ego

"Are vanity and egotism the result of knowledge or of ignorance? Egotism is of the nature of tamas; it is begotten by ignorance. On account of the barrier of ego one does not see God. All troubles come to an end when the ego dies."

(Gospel of Sri Ramakrishna)

Higher and Lower Austerities

"Hatha yoga is a form of austerity. But the hathayogi identifies himself with his body. His mind dwells on his body alone. But one can only understand the import of scriptures like the Bhagavata if one has studied the Nyaya, Vedanta, and Sankhya philosophies."

(Gospel of Sri Ramakrishna)

Drawn by God's Love

"If a man feels sincerely drawn to God, then God makes him practice disciplines. The devotee will certainly realize God if he practices them without desiring their results. A devotee observes many rites because of the injunctions of the scriptures. Such devotion is called vaidhi-bhakti. But there is a higher form of devotion called raga-bhakti, which springs from yearning and love for God. Prahlada had such devotion. When the devotee develops that love, he no longer needs to perform prescribed rites."

(Gospel of Sri Ramakrishna)

Envision the Truth

"When you think of Me, and meditate upon Me, you must think that all the sins committed by you in your several past lives have been burnt to ashes. You are now the pure, awakened, free Soul."

(The Compassionate Mother)

Divine Dreams, Verified Visions

"Is it so easy to have a divine vision, like of the Great Master? If you do a lot of japa and practice meditation, then you will be able to see Him. You may see Him even in a dream. Divine dreams are not illusory, especially in the early hours. Thereafter, one is not able to sleep anymore."

(The Compassionate Mother)

Free!

"The Master and I am always with you. This is the last birth for those who have received initiation from Me. Some of them may be born again, but they will merely come along with the Master."

(The Compassionate Mother)

Her Instructions

"Everyday after bathing, offer your salutations to the Master, then remember Him in the course of every piece of work that you do. Then you will be able to do all your duties very well. And this will fulfill the purpose of your japa and meditation. And when you find extra time, pray to Him whole-heartedly. Whatever you can do in the early hours, and before going to bed, do that much. Japa and meditation are meant for realizing God. It is only because you have received His grace that you have come here to Me."

(The Compassionate Mother)

Wisdom Facets From the Gem of Truth

Swami Vivekananda   Sri Ramakrishna's Disciples & Devotees

Congeniality of Love

"Love sees no distinction between man and man, between Aryan and Mlechcha, between a Brahmin and a Pariah, not even between a man and a woman. Love makes the whole universe as one's own home."

Abandoning Miracle-Mongering

"Why insist upon the telling of miracles with regards to God. They do not prove anything. Matter does not prove Spirit. What connection is there between the existence of God, soul, and immortality, and the working of miracles? Preach Sri Ramakrishna alone. Pass the cup that has satisfied your thirst. Do not disturb your head with metaphysical nonsense, and do not disturb others by your bigotry."

The School for Great Souls

"I have been dragged through a whole life of crosses and tortures. I have seen the nearest and dearest die, almost of starvation. I have been ridiculed, distrusted, and have suffered for my sympathy for the very men who scoff and scorn. Well, this is the school of misery, which is also the school for great souls and prophets for the cultivation of sympathy, of patience, and above all, of an indomitable iron will which quakes not even if the universe be pulverized at our feet."

Avatara Varishtaya

"No great idea can have a place in the heart unless one steps out of his little corner. Do you think that people of the West would be much attracted if I preached Hinduism? The very name of narrowness in ideas would scare them away! The real thing is the religion taught by Sri Ramakrishna. Always remember that Sri Ramakrishna came for the good of the world, not for a few, nor for name and fame. Spread only what He came to teach. Never mind for His name; it will spread itself." (All Selections, Letters of Vivekananda)

Sri Ramakrishna Gurudeva

"Where are light and hope? Where are assurance and solace in this all-engulfing darkness? They are in Sri Ramakrishna! Come from the elysian height of your unperturbed quiescence, beyond the maya of our troubled life tossed incessantly by poverty and pain, fear and anxieties, doubts and bewilderment. Come and stand before us, to awaken our drooping hearts, to lift us up and make us live in truth and balance." (Swami Virajananda, The Story of an Epoch)

Regain the Mind

"When people sometimes say to me, 'I find it so difficult to concentrate my mind; it goes to my business, to my household affairs, to my amusements, and it is impossible to hold it on any higher point.' 'Why is this?' I tell them. 'It is because your mind does not belong to you. You have sold it to your worldly interests. How can you expect to command what is not yours?'" (Swami Ramakrishnananda in Days in an Indian Monastery)

The Universal Spirit in Mankind

"Wherever there is expansion in love, or progress in well-being, individually or collectively, it springs, consciously or unconsciously, from the perception, the realization, and the putting into practice of the eternal truth of the universal spirit in man, and the oneness of all beings. This spiritual unity provides the continuity manifested throughout the ages in man's cultural and scientific development."
(Sw. Nityasvarupananda in Education for Human Unity & World Civilization)

Sadhana and Grace Go Hand in Hand

"The only thing necessary is to keep one's soul wide awake constantly by means of sadhana, and to remember that the jiva can taste the fruits of his sadhana only by God's grace."
(Nag Mahashaya in, A Saintly Householder Disciple of Sri Ramakrishna)

SCRIPTURAL SAYINGS
of the World's Religious Traditions

"The supreme gift is the gift of Truth; the supreme savior is the savior of Truth; the supreme delight is the delight of Truth, and the supreme illuminator is the Light of Truth. For, when the darkness envelops you, do you not seek for a lamp?"

"They who consent to the death of an animal, they who kill it, they who cut it up, the buyer, the seller, they who prepare its flesh, they who serve it up, and they who eat its flesh, are all to be regarded as having taken part in the murder. Those who abstain from all violence towards living beings, to the weak as to the strong, who kill not and who cause not to kill, those, I say, are Brahmins."

"I have strayed like a lost sheep seeking outside me what was within. I have run about the streets and places of the world, this great city, seeking Thee, but I have not found Thee because I sought Thee ill and came not to the place where Thou wert. Thou wert within me and I sought Thee without; Thou wert near and I sought Thee at a distance. If I had gone where Thou wert, I should immediately have met Thee."

"There are men in this world who labor to attain to spirituality, and sages who are pure and perfect who can explain this life and the next of which they themselves have intricate knowledge of."

"To truly love, one must have no reservations, but be prepared to cast oneself into the flame and to give up into it a hundred worlds. In this path there is no difference between good and evil; indeed, within the path of love, neither good nor evil exists anymore."

"Something beyond the power of our discrimination existed before Heaven and Earth. How profound is Its calm! How absolute is Its immateriality. It alone exists and does not change. It penetrates all and does not perish. It may be regarded as the mother of the universe. For myself, I know not Its name, but to give It a name I call It Tao."

Babaji Bob Kindler

MUMUKSHUTVAM
A Sincere and Authentic Desire for Freedom

One of the many great teachings in Vedanta centers around distinguishing between weak, middling, and strong detachment from the world in order to arrive at a mature desire for spiritual emancipation.

If asked about faith, the Vedantist has a quick and certain response. As the system of the Four Treasures and the Six Jewels (*Sadhanachatushtaya*) explains: faith, *shraddha*, is foundationally based in wise discrimination between the "unreal" and the "Real," between what is mutable and what is immutable. As Sri Krishna states, *"The unreal never is; the Real never ceases to be. The truth about both has been realized by the seers."* The spiritual aspirant possessing *viveka*, spiritual discrimination, carefully notes the difference between what changes and what remains the same, then lives and acts accordingly. Thus, viveka is sweet syllogism of the subtlest kind, but on purely spiritual levels. *"Separating the wheat from the chaff,"* the qualified seeker simply gleans all that is essential and leaves aside the nonessential. This wisdom way disabuses the intellect, debunks the conventional world, and circumvents egoistic intervention. In the end, in masterful attainment, it conduces to peace of mind, which is mandatory for achieving states of *samadhi*.

Spiritual Jewels and Treasures

Shraddha, the bedrock of faith, is much more than mere belief. It far exceeds blind faith, or assumed faith, although these may have their efficacy at early stages of inner seeking. This superlative quality proceeds directly from what Vedanta calls *samadhana*, the ability to concentrate — not just on tasks, or work, or fulfilling desires, or amassing wealth, or gaining success, or intellectual studies, or even on one's daily meditation. Transcending them all, it matures around that singular ability to concentrate on Reality alone, brooking no distractions. Shutting out, at will, all that is extraneous, the meditator in command of samadhana enters rapt communion with *Brahman*, free of the usual impediments (sleepiness, restlessness, brooding on duality, and attachment to bliss) that plague and impede other aspirants.

Samadhana, this special, singular concentration, in turn, depends upon the duo called *titiksha* and *uparati* for its attainment. Forbearing all ills and using them to develop inner strength is the aim of titiksha. Easing naturally into the atmosphere of self-settledness, or equanimity, is the way of attaining uparati. Titiksha is the result of knowing that *"suffering is,"* and helps in transcending it, and uparati proves to the mind that happiness is overrated, and that contentment is a much better station for consciousness to occupy.

Both titiksha and uparati emerge out of another duo called *sama* and *dama*, inner peace and self-control. As one of India's devotional wisdom songs states, *"There are highway robbers along the road of life. Be sure to keep the two sentinels, sama and dama, with you at all times."* The attainment of inner peace puts to death the problem of restless mind, and brooding mind, whereas self-control makes sure that they will never return again.

All of the aforementioned attributes, amassed, are called *Shatsampati*, The Six Jewels. Together they make up the third treasure of Vedanta and lead to the acquisition of pure faith, shraddha. The sequence looks like this: sama > dama > uparati > titiksha > samadhana = shraddha. This six-faceted third treasure is founded on the necessity of securing treasures one and two, *viveka* and *vairagya*. Viveka is discrimination between the Real, and the unreal, as mentioned above, and vairagya is detachment from the unreal once it has been uncovered. These are, again, the first two treasures. If these two treasures and the six jewels are sought after and attained, a pure desire for Freedom, *Mumukshutvam*, the fourth treasure, may follow; not until.

All of this exposes several crucial points pertinent to real spiritual progress. First, the mechanics of faith and its acquisition are clearly outlined, based upon sincere striving and intense yearning; and second, the rarity of attaining even a mere desire for Freedom, what to speak of absolute Freedom itself, is revealed. In spiritual life as cited by Vedanta, even a hint of a real desire for Freedom comes only after all this striving for inner character is accomplished. It is no wonder, then, and despite appearances, posturing, and pretending, that so few souls ever really develop an avid and ingenuous desire for lasting Freedom.

The Singular, Superlative Desire

Mumukshutvam, the real desire to be Free, is thus the fourth treasure of Vedanta. What to speak of securing it, there is still the need to act on it so as to experience freedom of an uninterrupted kind. Called *Moksha, Mukti, Nirvana, Samadhi,* and other noble appellations, spiritual freedom, as any non-dualist will tell you, is less of an acquisition or attainment and more of a rarefied atmosphere always at hand. Sometimes spoken of as a subtle presence, or a state of nondual abidance, its imminence is obscured by a diverse set of veils or coverings that are equally subtle.

Of course, the gross impediments are legion and legend. Souls laboring under the weights of lust, anger, jealousy, shame, pride, delusion, and the like (the six passions and the eight fetters), and suffering under the press of poisons such as stress, brooding, fear, and doubt, will seldom, if ever, consider the need to be free, what to speak of ever entertaining the thought of the possibility of an ultimate freedom of a spiritual nature. Since *"suffering is"* in this world, they will simply suffer, and will not attempt any escape from it. Moreover, since viveka is missing in such as these, any form of freedom that comes along will suffice, and will easily act as a fitting substitution for the real thing. The standard for freedom will thereby get lowered, generation by generation, century by century, age to age, its ideal thoroughly compromised as genuine spiritual qualities and the authentic practice which precedes them, fall by the wayside.

With this unfortunate sacrifice of spirituality in lieu of all that is worldly, i.e., seeking mammon instead of God, a host of substitutes get insidiously superimposed over Mumukshutvam. Masquerade is distraction, and humanity is all too ready to overlook the Real and embrace the unreal (because viveka is missing in them) in their mutual and ongoing thirst for the dream of life. At the physical and emotional level there is the problem of freedom from pain, freedom from suffering, and freedom from disease. On the social level is felt the need for freedom from conventional institutions and their limitations. On the political level there is the urge for freedom from oppression, freedom from tyranny, freedom from war and, ironically, freedom from politics. There is also the need to be free from religious rituals. In mankind's quest for a utopian society, all these imposters take over the collective awareness of humanity, and true Freedom — the only Freedom that has ever been and can ever be — is forgotten.

Where Real Freedom Resides

Spiritual life and its adherents, existing as if impervious to the trials and trammels of relative existence, are a world verily unto themselves. They are like an underground lava tube that extends from the top of the volcano to the flats below, transferring liquid fire to the ocean shore. That is, the Truth of Existence, rather than the question, "Does God exist?" has always been the main subject on the minds of the seers and sages, and they readily transmit this unadulterated message over the ages to any sincere soul who desires to hear it. In the midst of this congenial company is where Mumukshutvam abides, untouched by the discomfiting overlays of death, fear, doubt, and darkness, and those who live under their influence.

This divine dharma, and those who teach and follow it, are not easy to discover. A spiritual sangha is most often found under the auspices of a gracious guru. In the spiritual preceptor and the sincere souls who follow him, one will find living examples of Mumukshutvam.

But the guru is not popular in this day and time, because the church has taken his place. However, spirituality cannot be gotten from churches, books, and clergy; it must be gotten from a luminary. Where else? However, it is highly unlikely that even sound religion can be secured in today's tepid religious climate, and spirituality is a far sight beyond authentic religion. Therefore, the avid soul in pursuit of Truth will have to develop some unusual powers of subtle scrutiny in order to find out those special locations and atmospheres where matters of the Spirit are called forth and spoken of, as if in secret. If the fortunate soul can penetrate into these inner circles, the amazing spectacle of true lovers of God will be revealed unto him.

> "....the Truth of Existence, rather than the question, "Does God exist?" has always been the main subject on the minds of the seers and sages, and they readily transmit this unadulterated message over the ages to any sincere soul who desires to hear it. In the midst of this congenial company is where Mumukshutvam abides...."

The Congenial Countenance of Mumukshutvam

The face of pure desire is most endearing, and unlike any that the freshly seeking soul, used to the crass appearances of the world, has ever beheld. To worldly people, anything thought of or talked about in the name of religion and spirituality amounts to mere persiflage. Even when these otherwise sensitive subjects come into the hands of the intellectuals and priests, they only end up, at best, as well-presented sophistry. What kind of fair treatment can religion expect in the hands of such as these? They have sold out any allegiance they may have once held to the Truth, and are now only peddling compromised dualism for selfish purposes and manipulative reasons. *"This is merely religious shopkeeping,"* said Swami Vivekananda when he came to the West and beheld the state of religion here.

But all this only makes the countenance of Mumukshutvam all the more attracting to the sincere seeker. At first, the appearance of a true desire for Freedom may be somewhat startling to the sincere soul who is awakening from the hazy sleep of maya. Conditioned over lifetimes by ingesting the thin, sour, gruel of relativity, foisted upon them by a dharma-less upbringing, a materialistic society, worldly friends and relatives, and conventional religion, newly aspiring souls cannot yet appreciate that singular Freedom which has so easily divested itself of forms and objects. Yet, *"Only renunciation is fearless,"* runs the line of a famous stotram of India. Where renunciation is natural, there, the face of a pure desire for Freedom will shine most brightly.

Imagine, then, the wonder of a rare desire that holds not the slightest trace of hypocrisy in it, that contains no hankering after the things of the world, that has reached the state of world-weariness wherein no return to mundane matters is even possible. As Swami Vivekananda has so beautifully put it, *"What reason is there for me to conform to the vagaries of the world around me and not obey the voice of Truth within? Neither numbers, nor powers, nor wealth, nor learning, nor eloquence, nor anything else will prevail, but purity, living the life, in one word, anubhuti, realization."*

On the chart of the facing page, the meaning of the word "Freedom" gets revealed, courtesy of the ancient rishis of India who realized it in deep meditation and returned to tell of It.

The True Meaning of Moksha/Mukti

"The Soul is not purified by the six-limbed Yoga; nor is It made pure by the destruction of the mind's waves; neither is it rendered pure by bowing at the guru's feet. The Soul is pure by its very nature."

— *Avadhuta Gita*

↓ The Free Soul – Jivanmukta ↓

→ Lives in the mortal physical frame as Brahman

→ Sports in the world as the playground of Shakti

→ Sees the universe as transcendental Consciousness

→ Views all objects as representations of AUM

Mukti Is Not Liberation from Bondage:

1) Is not freedom which is produced or generated →
   * not freedom from senses
   * not freedom from passion
   * not freedom from nature
   * not freedom from desire
   * not freedom from sin

2) Is not a result of evolution, development, or transformation →
   * not the solving of problems
   * not brought about by some power above or outside
   * not the disappearance of weakness or imperfections

3) Is not something to be attained →
   * not the result of movement away from one's Source

4) Is not something to be realized via purification →
   * not due to the soul's fall from its original status
   * not because the world is corrupt or needs escaping
   * not because the soul has gathered impurities

"Mukti or moksha is not to be considered a state or experience yet to come. It is the eternal condition of the Self, which is nothing other than Brahman." — *Shankaracharya*

Chart by Babaji Bob Kindler — Property of SRV Associates

The essential message that this chart means to communicate is that true Freedom is a condition ever at hand. "Fire-darting reformists" have it that if one can get rid of desire, be free from passion, rise above the senses, transcend nature, or repent their sins, then freedom will be the result. Seekers after heavenly existence put their hopes for freedom on a Power outside or above them, or they have made the mistake of moving away from their source and all will be righted when they return. Those laboring under the darksome mantle of transgressions feel that freedom will come when they reassume their due and rightful status after having fallen from grace. Those taking refuge in psychological methodologies and its aims presume that the solving of problems will result in freedom, that when weaknesses and imperfection go, freedom will suddenly be there.

But all of these views have failed to comprehend the true nature of Freedom. Only the realized seer knows Freedom, and that especial knowledge has shown him that 1, it is never produced or generated; 2, it does not come about via evolution, via the passage of time, or by seeming transformations; 3, it does not occur due to any regimen of purification and, 4, it cannot be attained by practices and self-effort. *"It is, and It is to be realized."*

What the Four Treasures Can Purchase

If Mumukshutvam has any final aim at all, it is this: to usher in the possibility, and finally the complete assurance, of direct spiritual experience, as rare as it is. As Ramprasad Sen of Bengal puts it, *"The lover of sublime Kali gazes intently, tears pouring down like monsoon rain. Only these most precious raindrops can quench the desperate thirst of the heart, that rare winged creature who drinks water only from the heavens, never from earthly springs, lakes, or streams."* Thus, the sublime and secret rewards of spiritual experience are incomparable, but only those who have realized the ultimate desirability of it will ever know this fact.

And this fleshes out the content and description of Mumukshutvam — a pure desire for Reality alone. To explain it from the opposite side, this strong inner urge for Freedom is not sought by souls who are attracted to wealth, who are keen for personal power, who are vainglorious in their egos, or who are tied inexorably to house, home, spouse, and progeny. To those bound into matter, and exceedingly fond of their physical bodies, matters pertaining to spirituality, to real Freedom, are far too recondite to even consider. Thus, Truth, originally meant to be revealed and given to all, remains an esoteric subject in minds that, what to speak of lacking enough strength and conviction to seek It out, eventually come to even doubt Its very existence.

The seer possessing Mumukshutvam receives far more than a single spiritual experience. His mental, intellectual, and philosophical foundations get firmly set; they become unassailable. Beings sit and stare in amazed wonder at his unswerving resolve, the depth and profundity of his exacting perceptions, and his unbridled exuberance for nondual Truth and Awareness. As the saying states, *"He has the courage of his convictions."* From this platform such qualities and attributes as empathy, wisdom, compassion, and service, are a given; they are as if tangible, their immediate presence, palpable. It is here that a real teacher of humanity, even of the gods, is born.

The Bliss of Freedom

For all of these powerful reasons, then, the great soul departs the marketplace of convention where the subtle wealth of his Four Treasures go unrecognized. He enters into the divine, internal *"Mart of Joy,"* where he purchases his own freedom, once and for all time. Nor is he necessarily satisfied with this translucent *"Pearl of Great Price,"* but re-enters the mundane realm to shine Its incandescent Light on other souls. Some run away at first sight of It. Others approach out of curiosity, then wander away, caught up in the hypnotism of various distractions around them. A few, however, recognize something of infinite value, and swiftly gather around. To such ready souls as these, the luminary dispenses the ignorance and misery-destroying message of Advaita, found nowhere else on earth but in a realized soul.

To become emulous of a luminary in possession of ultimate Freedom, as well as the Wisdom to attain it, is most noble. There can hardly be a calling as beneficial and auspicious as this, in any world, at any level of consciousness. As Sri Krishna puts it in the Bhagavad Gita, *"That one who, with supreme devotion to Me, will teach this immensely profound philosophy to my devotees, shall doubtless come to Me alone. Nor is there any among beings who renders dearer service to Me than he, nor shall there be another on earth dearer to Me than he. Through him I am worshipped by Jnana Yajna, the best of sacrifices, such is my firm conviction."*

What to speak of joining this great luminary in the work of awakening sleeping souls, the devotee or disciple can work on his or her own realization of Freedom and, in such precious and congruent atmosphere, perfect the inner vision by which his own singular pathway to innate perfection is uncovered, navigated, and mastered. Then, looking back, he sees that it all began with a single, ardent, pure, and veracious desire for ultimate emancipation, called Mumukshutvam by the seers — far transcendent of ordinary human desires, and never to be underrated by the soul seeking liberation from the ignoble trammels of Maya.

Babaji Bob Kindler is the Spiritual Director of the SRV Associations with centers in Hawaii, Oregon, and California. A teacher of religion and spirituality and a prolific author, his books include *The Avadhut, Twenty-Four Aspects of Mother Kali, Ten Divine Articles of Sri Durga, Sri Sarada Vijnanagita, Swami Vivekananda Vijnanagita, An Extensive Anthology of Sri Ramakrishna's Stories, A Quintessential Yoga Vasishtha,* and *Reclaiming Kundalini Yoga.* Founder and Artistic Director of Jai Ma Music, he is also an accomplished musician and composer who has produced over twenty-five albums of instrumental and devotional music to date.

Ladder of Spiritual Ascent
(continued from page 18)

karmas, e.g. turning an evil karma to bear an advantageous fruit

5. *apurvabandha* — minimizing the duration and intensity of fruition of karmas being performed in the present time (*kriyamana karma*)

9th Stage: Anivrttikarana Gunasthana

The aspirant ascends to this stage by suppressing or destroying all lustful desires, which in Jainism are called *veda*, and all passions (except subtle greed).

10th Stage: Sukshma Samparaya Gunasthana

In this stage the remaining six no-kasayas (hasya, rati, arati, bhaya, shoka and ghrna: laughter, attachment, aversion, fear, sorrow and hatred) are removed.

11th Stage: Upashanta-Moha Gunasthana

This unfortunate, dangerous, and necessarily impermanent stage is reached when the last of the twenty-eight mohaniya karmas responsible for subtle greed (*samjvalana lobha*) is suppressed. Samjvalana lobha is interpreted by some scholars as deep-rooted attachment to the body, and clinging to life. Since the subtle aspects of evil tendencies are merely suppressed, they reawaken and the aspirant slips back to the seventh stage after 48 minutes.

12th Stage: Kshina-Moha Gunasthana

Aspirants progressing by annihilating the evil tendencies go to this stage directly from the tenth. This is the stage of moral perfection when all *caritra mohaniya* karmas are destroyed, and is also called *yathakhyata caritra*. The soul remains in this stage for 48 minutes only.

13th stage: Sayogi-Kevali Gunasthana

During the last part of the twelfth stage, *darsanavaraniya*, *jnanavaraniya*, and *antaraya karmas* are also destroyed and the individual no more remains a struggling aspirant. He becomes a *kevali*, an omniscient one, and obtains perfect faith, bliss and power. The four aghati karmas however remain owing to which physical, mental, and vocal activities called yoga continue but which do not entail bondage. A person in this stage is also called *arhat* or *sarvajna* and is equivalent to the *jivanmukta* of Vedanta.

14th stage: Ayogi-Kevali Gunasthana

With the natural exhaustion of aghati karmas which are responsible for the specific body, stipulated duration of life and experiences, the soul attains this stage of perfect freedom. He is now a siddha. The duration of this stage is the shortest, equivalent to the time required to pronounce the five short vowels of the Sanskrit alphabet. It is called ayogi because there is absence of all physical, vocal, and mental activity, which in Jainism is called yoga. This stage compares well with the videha-mukti of Vedanta [freedom from all forms].

Summary

According to Jainism there are five conditions of bondage: perversity of attitude (*mithyatva*), non-abstinence from sense-pleasures and violence (*avirati*), spiritual inertia or carelessness (*pramada*), passions or evil tendencies (*kasaya*), and the threefold activity of the body, speech, and mind (*yoga*). Of these, mithyatva is the first to go in the fourth stage of samyag drsti. Lay and monastic vows in the fifth and sixth stages eliminate avirati. Pramada is removed in the seventh stage. The destruction of the four kasayas takes the longest way. Starting from the fourth stage it is completed in the twelfth stage. Finally, the threefold yoga ends in the last stage.

Of the four types of thinking (dhyana), rudra dhyana persists up to the sixth stage. This means that even after taking monastic vows, undesirable thoughts may persist. Arta dhyana, undesirable thinking dominated by sorrow and depression, may persist up to the eleventh stage. Dharma dhyana starts in the fourth (and third) stage, and reaches its culmination in the eleventh. The aspirant is able to do the first of the four types of pure thinking (sukla dhyana) in the seventh stage, but is able to take up its second type only in the twelfth stage. These two meditations are based on scriptural texts. In the thirteenth stage, the kevali does the third type, sukla dhyana, and liberation is attained by the fourth type in the final stage.

A review of the duration spent in each stage shows that the aspirant stays for the longest period in the fourth, fifth, and sixth gunasthanas. These therefore are given great importance and described in greater detail in Jain scriptures. The eighth, although a very important stage, lasts for a short period only. The five-fold technique described in that stage can be applied repeatedly from the sixth to the tenth stage for the rapid elimination of karmas.

This brief review may be concluded by reminding the readers that descriptions are necessarily imperfect, and that these stages are better understood via practice and actual experience.

The author wishes to express his gratefulness to Dr. Sagarmal Jain, director of the Parsvanath Jain Research Institute, Varanasi, for guiding and scrutinizing this work.

A former editor of the Vedanta Keshari, and previously of the Ramakrishna Mission Home of Service, Swami Brahmeshananda is a senior monk of the Ramakrishna Order and until recently was the Secretary of the Ramakrishna Mission Ashrama in Chandigarh, India. Over the years his writings in Hindi and English have appeared in several journals, including Prabuddha Bharata, Vedanta Keshari, and Nectar of Nondual Truth. He specializes in themes related to Jainism. He is now retired and living in Varanasi.

◆ *Rabbi Rami Shapiro*

ESSENTIALS OF JUDAISM

Divinity, Scripture, & Community in the Hearts and Minds of the Jewish People

Every world religion should possess and display an open testament to its redeeming facets and features, a kind of manual of self-explanation that offers to its adherents and devotees the main aspects of its overall composition. Here, this very kind of synopsis has been rendered for Judaism, inclusive of its harmonious similarities with Indian Religion and Philosophy, and its fundamental differences from Christianity.

In this essay I will focus on Jewish ideas about God, Torah, and Israel (Divinity, Scripture, Community), that shape the minds and hearts of Jews, and give form to our yearning for God and godliness. It is important to note that Jews lack a central authority. Each of our rabbis (rabbi means "my master") are empowered to interpret Judaism as she or he deems fit, and there is no one Judaism that is definitive. All authentic Jewish thinking, however, must be rooted in the texts and teachings of our tradition.

God

Judaism offers many names for God, but the three most important ones are Elohim, YHVH, and Ain Sof.

Elohim

Elohim is a plural noun literally translated as "gods" (El is the singular). The plural is used to remind us that God manifests as the diversity of nature: God *"fills and surrounds all worlds"* (Zohar III:225a); God *"surrounds all, and fills all, and is the life of all; You are in All"* (Hymn of Glory, 12th century).

Further linking Elohim to the manifest world, Rabbi Abraham Abulafia (1240–1291) noted that the numerical value of Elohim, God (aleph/1 + lamed/30 + heh/5 + yod/10 + mem/40) equaled that of Hateva, Nature (heh/5 + tet/9 + bait/2 + ayin/70), with each word adding up to 86. Words with the same numerical value were thought to be synonyms, thus Abulafia taught that Nature is God manifest in time and space. This does not mean, of course, that God is reduced to Nature, but that Nature is a part of God.

YHVH

If Elohim is God manifest as all form, Saguna Brahman if you like, YHVH is the unmanifest God, Nirguna Brahman. Because the word YHVH is unpronounceable (both literally, lacking vowels, and traditionally in that Jews are forbidden to speak the name of God), our rabbis decreed that whenever YHVH appears in our texts we are to read Adonai instead. Adonai means Lord, reflecting the bias of the ancient men who first used the word in reference to God. English translations of the Bible that use "Lord" are not translating YHVH, but its substitute. YHVH itself is not a noun, but a verb – a variant of the Hebrew verb, "to be." YHVH is not a being or even a Supreme Being, but Being itself.

Ain Sof

Ain Sof (literally Without, Ain, and End, Sof) is the Infinite Godhead, the God beyond God. Ain Sof is the infinite field of play in which all life and death happens. This is pure Godhead without attributes and form that yet embraces all attributes and form. Here are some of the teachings that reflect this understanding of God:

"There is no place devoid of God." (Tikkunei Zohar 57)

"God fills everything and God is everything." (Rabbi Joseph Gikatilla, 1248–1305)

"God is above and below, in heaven and on earth, and there is no existence beside God." (Moshe de Leon, 1250–1305)

"If asked, 'Does anything exist outside of God?' the answer would be, 'Nothing exists outside of God.' If asked, 'How did God bring forth being from nothingness, for there is a great difference between the two?' the answer would be, 'God lacks nothing, neither being nor nothingness, for being is in nothingness and nothingness is being.'" *(Rabbi Azriel of Gerona, 1160-1238)*

"Everything is in God, and God is in everything and beyond everything, and there is nothing besides God." (Moses Cordovero, 1522–1570)

"Where can I find You — and where can I not find You, Moses?
Above — only You; below — only You;
To the east — only You; to the west — only You;
To the south — only You; to the north— only You;
If it is good — it is You; if it is not good — also You;
It is You; it is only You."
(Rabbi Levi Yitzchak of Berdichev, 1740–1810)

This nondual (advaitic) understanding of God is succinctly stated by Rabbi Yitzhak of Homel, a 19th century sage who wrote in Yiddish, the language of European Jews, and summed up our teaching this way, "Es is mehr nito vie Ehr alein un vider kehren altz is Gott; There is nothing but God alone and, once again, all is God."

Godliness

There is nothing in Judaism that corresponds to God manifesting as Krishna or Jesus. But Judaism does teach that human beings are the *"image and likeness of God"* (Genesis 1:26), each one of us a reflection of God and capable of manifesting godli-

> "....but Judaism does teach that human beings are the *"image and likeness of God"* (Genesis 1:26), each one of us a reflection of God and capable of manifesting godliness, which we define as justice and compassion to all beings."

ness, which we define as justice and compassion to all beings. *"You know humanity what it is that YHVH requires of you — do justly, love compassion, and walk humbly with your God"* (Micah 6:8). Indeed, Judaism is essentially nothing but a series of practices for doing just that.

Torah

Torah means "instruction," and in its broadest context refers to written and oral revelations received by Moses on Mount Sinai 2600 years ago, as well as the body of interpretive work by rabbis since then. These come down to us in a variety of books:

TaNaKH

TaNaKH refers to the Hebrew Bible, and is an acronym for *Torah* (the Five Books of Moses), *Nevi'im* (Prophets), and *Ketuvim* (Writings). Torah contains ancient parables, narratives featuring the founders of our faith, like Abraham and Sarah, and their children and grandchildren, the story of our liberation from slavery in Egypt under Moses, who was our greatest prophet, as well as priestly laws and codes, ethical teachings, and ritual practices. Nevi'im contain the teachings of our prophets after Moses, and focuses primarily on issues of justice and compassion. Nevi'im also contains Judaism's hope for a future in which nations *"....shall beat their swords into plowshares and their spears into pruning hooks. Nation shall not take up sword against nation; neither shall they know war any more. Rather all people shall sit under their grapevines or fig trees with no one to make them afraid."* (Micah 4:34). Ketuvim is a collection of diverse writings from the most devotional (Psalms) to the most philosophical (Job).

Talmud

The Talmud (learning) is the anthology of a thousand years of rabbinic teachings on Jewish life, law, lore, biblical commentary, civic obligations, and ethics. The purpose of the Talmud is to apply the principles of TaNaKH to the realities of everyday life.

The oldest part of the Talmud is the *Mishnah* (repeat), oral teachings handed down from rabbi to rabbi over many generations, and memorized through verbal repetition. The earliest texts of the Mishnah date to around 500 BCE. Mishnah was committed to writing in the 3rd century CE when, due to the exile of the Jews throughout the Roman Empire, our rabbis feared the teachings would be lost.

The second part of the Talmud is the *Gemara*, which is essentially an extension of and commentary on the Mishnah. The Gemara was committed to writing in by the middle of the 6th century CE, again to prevent the loss and corruption of the teaching. The Talmud contains 67 separate books of rabbinic teachings.

Midrash

Jews believe that Torah is a living document continually revealing new insights when approached with creativity and imagination. *Midrashim* (plural of midrash from the Hebrew word drash, "to investigate") are these insights, some dealing with legal issues, others with ethical and moral matters. Collections of midrashim, some dating back to the last centuries BCE, were first compiled in the 5th century CE, and new midrashim continue to be written today. Indeed one of the central practices of rabbis is to investigate the teachings and texts of Torah and to find new meanings in them.

Zohar

Zohar (Book of Splendor) is a 13th century CE compilation of mystical teachings on Torah revealed through the adventures and insights of the 2nd century mystic, Rabbi Shimon bar Yohai and his circle of disciples. Zohar is highly esoteric, and to understand properly requires a thorough knowledge of both Torah and Talmud. While many Jews have heard of Zohar, few have read it, and fewer still understand it.

The essential thing to know about Jewish texts is that they are living documents meant to be sources of ever new revelation and insight. We believe these are holy books, and because they are holy they cannot be frozen in time or imprisoned behind the bars of any one interpretation. On the contrary, we must continually free them from the past that they might speak to the present. This naturally results in a host of often conflicting readings of the same text, and how we handle these conflicts gives one deep insight into the Jewish mind.

Elu v'Elu

Jewish education is rooted in a single principle: *elu v'elu divrei Elohim Chayyim*. These opinions (elu) and these opposing opinions (v'elu), no matter how opposite or even mutually exclusive, are both the words of the Living God (divrei Elohim Chayyim). Because God is infinite, the Word of God has infinite meanings. To access these meanings we must use imagination as well as reason.

Therefore, study in Judaism is not simply a matter of learning the insights of a master (rabbi), but learning the principles of investigation (drash) that you might find fresh insights of your own. The goal of a rabbi is not just to pass on the teachings of others, but to educate students to the point where they can discover meanings for themselves. We call this "raising up of disciples," meaning that we are to raise them up to surpass us with their own imagination, creativity, and insight.

This results in a vast array of different and often contradictory meanings. Rather than seek to harmonize the differences and remove contradiction, Judaism revels in them. Rather then seek to articulate one set of right views, rabbis train Jews to hold, value, and respect as many different and even contradictory views as they can. Indeed, the more intellectual dissonance one can embrace, the more intelligent one is said to be. While Judaism values consistency in matters of morality, it finds consistency an impediment in matters of intellectual development.

Chevruta Study

While solitary study isn't prohibited, Jews are taught that study with a friend or partner (*chaver*) is preferred. Chevruta or partner study is rooted in dialogue, argument, and debate. Together you and your chaver explore a given text or teaching. Each of you brings your best thoughts to bear on the matter, supporting your view with the teachings of the sages and texts from the tradition. Your task is not to convince your partner of the rightness of your argument, but to help him or her understand it so well that she can convincingly make the argument herself. She may prefer her own position, but she can understand and see the merit of your position. And, of course, you are to come into the same relationship with your partner's position as well. We call this relationship *ezer k'nego*, literally "one who helps through opposition."

Because chevruta study is dialogical, it is done out loud with each partner presenting arguments and counter arguments in a chanted singsong fashion that aids one's capacity to remember and repeat the argument being made. First time visitors to a traditional Jewish classroom are often shocked by the seeming chaos of the process. Everyone is singing their arguments, often jumping up to retrieve another text or to pick someone else's brain in a wild, joyous, and, for us, sacred dance of the mind that, if done well, can lead to a holy awakening of the heart and soul.

The role of the rabbi in this setting is not to settle the arguments but to fuel them. There is no settlement: *elu v'elu*, both sides are right, and it is the process that matters.

Israel

Israel (Yisrael) refers to the global family of Jews, the State of Israel, and the Jewish spiritual mindset. I will speak briefly of each, but it is the latter that matters most to this essay.

Israel as Family

Jews are not a race or ethnicity. There are Jews of every race, and Jews of every ethnicity. There are African Jews, Arabic Jews, Indian Jews, Chinese Jews, Mongolian Jews, Japanese Jews, South American Jews, North American Jews, Western, Central, Eastern European Jews, and more. Nor are we a single linguistic community. While our holy books are written and studied in Hebrew (often with the aid of translations), there are many other Jewish languages such as Yiddish (Judeo-German), Ladino (Judeo-Spanish), Judeo-Arabic, and Judeo-Persian. In Cochin, in the Indian state of Kerala, the Jews speak Judeo-Malayalam.

The best way to understand the nature of the Jewish people is to imagine a global family with a common ancestry, literature, liturgy, and history that, primarily through forced exile and expulsions, have spread throughout the world.

Jews first arrived in India, for example, as traders during the time of King Solomon (10th century BCE). With the destruction of our Temple in Jerusalem and the exile of Jews by the Babylonians in 596 BCE, more of us came to South India as refugees. When the Romans destroyed the Temple in 70 CE, the Jews were again exiled, and again many of us found our way to India.

Jews were welcome in India, and a still extant set of copper plates called the Sasanam codified the relationship of the Indian kings with the Jewish people. The Jews were granted the right to live freely in South India, to build synagogues, own property "without conditions," and to do so "for as long as the world and moon exist." Hindu India has been very good to us, and the decline of the Chochin Jewish community has to do with communal in-fighting and, since 1948, the desire to return to their homeland in Israel, rather than any anti-Jewish prejudice on the part of India herself.

As with any extended family, Jews differ on many things, including what it means to be Jewish. While we all tell the same historical tales, read the same holy books, pray the same prayers, and revere the same prophets and sages, we differ widely as to what these all mean and how we are to embody the teachings they contain. Sometimes our differences become fixed in competing denominations, from the most fundamentalist and nationalistic, to the most liberal and cosmopolitan. And yet we are all and always Jews.

Israel as a State

Jews are Zionists. Zion is a hill in the city of Jerusalem, and today the word refers both to Jerusalem and to the State of Israel as a whole. To be a Zionist means to believe in the Jewish people's right to an independent Jewish State in the Land of Israel. Jews will differ as to the boundaries of the state, and how best to establish and govern it, but few Jews are actually opposed to the idea of a free Jewish state.

Talk of the State of Israel can get very heated. What Jews see as a moment of liberation and return home, Palestinians see as the *Nakba*, "the Catastrophe" that exiled thousands from their ancestral lands. Both peoples are correct.

While Jews were fleeing to a new state that welcomed them, Palestinians were left in limbo. Today, over sixty years later, the dream of Palestinian statehood has yet to be fulfilled. This is in no small part due to the machinations of politicians — Israeli, Arab, European, and American — who find it more conducive to their own political agendas to maintain the horror of Palestinian statelessness, than to push toward justice and a Palestinian State alongside Israel.

Zionism and Racism

In 1975, by a vote of 72 to 35, the United Nations General Assembly, under economic and political pressure from oil rich Muslim states and their allies, passed Resolution 3379 declaring that Zionism was a form of racism. The resolution was repealed in 1991, but the charge that Zionism is racism, persists. It is a false one.

Zionism is the Jewish people's liberation movement. Our concern is to protect a free Jewish state and not deprive any other people of their own state. From a Zionist perspective there is no reason why the freedom of one people requires the disempowerment of another. That said, Zionism has been and continues to be used by Jewish extremists in and out of the Israeli government to excuse terrible acts of discrimination against Palestinians. We see something similar in militant Indian nationalists and Hindu fundamentalists, yet no one would take from this the notion that Hinduism is intrinsically racist.

To declare Zionism to be racism is an act of terror against the Jewish people designed to delegitimize not only the State of Israel, but the Jewish people themselves. There is nothing intrinsic to Zionism, Judaism, Jews, Israelis, Islam, Palestinians, or Palestinian hopes for statehood that prevents the establishment of a free and independent Palestine side by side the Jewish State of Israel. What stands in the way of liberation is politics and the fear, greed, anger, and hatred that infects the minds and hearts of too many people — not only in the Middle East but around the globe.

Israel as a State of Mind

The word *yisrael* (Israel) means "one who wrestles with God and survives." The term comes to us through our ancestor Jacob, whom, we are told, wrestled with God as the final stage of his transformation into a great leader (Genesis Chapter 32).

According to legend, Jacob masqueraded as his elder brother, Esau, to deceive his father and wrest control of the family from his brother. The ruse worked, but Esau pledged to murder his brother in retaliation. Jacob fled for his life, and in so doing began a long process of maturation that ultimately brought him to his encounter with God.

By then Jacob had two wives, and many children, servants, cattle, goats, and sheep. Leaving his father in law's employ (and defense) to return home, Jacob learned that his brother Esau was racing toward him with a small army of highly trained warriors. Having grown far beyond the narcissism, cowardice, and trickery of his youth, Jacob took his family and household to safety and went out to meet his brother alone and unarmed.

That night, as he awaited the army of Esau, an angel attacked him, and the two wrestled until dawn. Neither could defeat the other, though the angel did wound Jacob's hip, causing him to limp for the rest of his life. At dawn the angel demanded an end to the conflict, but Jacob would only agree on the condition that the angel bless him.

The blessing was in fact a change of spiritual status symbolized by the giving of a new name. No longer would Jacob be called Jacob, "usurper," but Yisrael, one who wrestles with God and survives (Genesis 32:29).

At the moment the angel departed, Esau arrived with his warriors. As the two brothers approached one another it was clear that something had changed. Seeing his brother Esau's anger melt, and the two men embraced and wept in reconciliation. This is the first sign of what it is to be Yisrael/Israel: compassion triumphs over anger.

After a time, Esau invited Jacob/Yisrael to gather his family and his household and return home with him. Jacob declined, and his reason for doing so is the second sign of what it is to be Yisrael. Jacob said to Esau, "You travel at the pace of the warrior, while I walk as a nursing mother with her young" (Genesis 33:13). Yisrael is not a warrior, but a nurse and nurturer. This is the dual mindset of Yisrael — one who both wrestles with the All-Powerful, and yet is devoted to the welfare of the powerless.

The Purpose of the Jew

Our people were born in an act of radical trust. Without any introduction or preparation, an elderly couple, Abram and Sarai, were challenged by an unknown God to leave their country, their kin, and their parents, and travel to an unstated destination (Genesis 12:1). And they did so without hesitation.

The Hebrew Bible tells us that the actual command of God was *lech lecha*, a phrase that literally means "walk (lech) toward oneself (lecha)." Our rabbis teach that the journey of Abram and Sarai (soon to be called Abraham and Sarah) was both an outer journey toward the Land of Israel, and an inner journey from the conditioned self — the self shaped by nationalism, ethnicity, tribe, and family (the very things God asks them to leave behind) to the unconditional Self that sees all things as manifestations of the One.

While God did not tell Abram and Sarai where they were to go, God did tell them why: *"Through you all the families of the earth will be blessed"* (Genesis 12:3). The purpose of Yisrael, the purpose of the Jewish people, is to be a blessing to all the families of the earth — human, animal, plant, and mineral. We are to live life in such a way as to be of benefit to all beings. At its best, Judaism is the way the Jew lives as a blessing.

Judaism as a Spiritual Path

The purpose of spiritual practice is to see through the illusion of self to the reality of Self. The Self we are talking about is called *mochin d'gadlut*, spacious mind, a mind open to the highest levels of consciousness — *Chayyah*, and *Yechidah*, which are roughly equivalent to the Vedanta's *Ishvara-Chaitanya* and *Brahma-Chaitanya*, respectively.

Spacious mind is contrasted to *mochin d'katnut*, or narrow mind, which is locked into *neshamah* — the egoic self similar to the *ahamkara* of Vedanta. Neshamah sees itself to be apart from God, while Chayyah knows itself to be a part of God, and Yechidah is the Divine Consciousness flowing to both spacious and narrow minds.

Other aspects of mind include *Nefesh* and *Ruach*, with similarities to *Saksi-Chaitanya* in Vedanta. As in Vedanta, these distinctions of consciousness are not absolute and arise from human limitations (*upadhis*), and not from any actual division in *Yechidah/Brahma-Chaitanya* itself.

In Vedanta we speak of the four yogas: karma, bhakti, raja, and jnana. While Judaism doesn't differentiate its practices in this way, it actually makes matters clearer if we do. So I will use the four yogas model to help explain Judaism as a spiritual path.

Halakhah: The Way of Action (Karma Yoga)

The Hebrew word, *halakhah*, means "path," and refers to the traditions a Jew observes as he or she walks (halakh) through life. Traditionally, Jews speak of 613 *mitzvot* (holy deeds; mitzvah is the singular) at the core of Jewish practice. Many of these deeds can only be done in the Jerusalem Temple, an institution that was destroyed two thousand years ago. Among the hundreds that remain, however, the goal is always the same — to attune body, heart, and mind to the presence of God (*Shekhinah*) in, with, and as all things.

Of the hundreds of mitzvot, let me mention but three: *Shabbat*, *Kashrut*, and *Gemilut Chasadim*.

Every seven days Jews make Shabbat, and retreat from the world of work into the world of contemplation, study, and prayer. For us, Shabbat is like a weekly taste of sannyasa.

The key to Kashrut (ethical consumption) is a respect for life and a commitment to the reduction of suffering. The original human diet as laid out in Genesis was strictly vegetarian. According to Torah, humans only began to eat animals after the Flood (Genesis chapters 6 through 9) when the earth was too wet to plant. Aptly, it is only then that animals are said to fear humans (Genesis 9:2).

Judaism allows for the eating of certain animals, and forbids the eating of most. Even eating permitted animals is quite difficult. First, Judaism forbids killing animals except for food. Second, animal slaughter must be done only in a ritual context designed to minimize the suffering of the animal, and only by a righteous and pious person specially trained in kosher slaughtering (which is why Jews are prohibited from hunting). Third, Jews are forbidden to mix meat and dairy even to the point of having to have separate pots, dishes, and utensils for each. If you will pardon the pun, the point of kashrut (kosher) is and was to make the eating of meat rare at best.

But food alone does not speak to the full reality of keeping kosher. Anything produced by exploited workers, or produced in a manner that wantonly squanders the earth's resources is considered unfit for Jewish consumption as well. While mostly associated with dietary rules, keeping kosher is the practice of lifting all our consumption to the highest ethical and environmental standards we can achieve.

Gemilut Chasadim

Gemilut chasadim are personal acts of kindness that one does throughout the day. Three examples of this are *shmirat ha-lashon*, literally guarding your speech against falsehood, exaggeration, and gossip; *tzedakah*, practicing generosity toward the poor; and *bikkur kholim*, visiting the sick.

Teffilah: The Way of Devotion (Bhakti Yoga)

Traditionally, Jews are to pray communally three times each day: morning, early afternoon, and evening. In addition, there are specific private prayers to be recited when you awake in the morning and when you go to sleep at night, and individuals are encouraged to recite 100 blessings of thanksgiving throughout the day. The purpose of prayer is to cultivate gratitude and love.

Hitbonenut: The Way of Contemplation (Raja Yoga)

While there are many meditation techniques in Judaism, one most familiar to Hindus would be our version of mantra and japam. Perhaps the most common Name of God for recitation is *HaRachaman* (the Compassionate One), and the most used Hebrew mantra are *Ein od milvado* ("there is nothing but God"), and *Shiviti YHVH l'negdi tamid* ("I see God manifest before me always"). We are taught that "*a person should be so absorbed in this practice (of repeating mantra) that there is no longer awareness of self. There is nothing but the flow of life; all thoughts are with God. One who still knows how intensely goes the practice has not yet overcome the bonds of self*" (Dov Baer, 1773–1827).

Limmud: The Way of Wisdom (Jnana Yoga)

I have already written about the limmud, study. Now let me share with you a bit more of the process. The purpose of limmud is the realization of God. We call this *PaRDeS*, Paradise, an acronym made up of the first letter of each of the four elements of study: *Peshat, Remez, Drash*, and *Sod*. Peshat ("simple") is the literal reading of a text, or the simple presentation of an argument. Remez ("hint") refers to aspects of the text or cracks in the argument that hint at something greater than the Peshat or surface reading allows. Drash ("investigate") applies reason, imagination, and intuition to these openings in order to see where they might lead. Sometimes the drash process becomes so deep that you experience a direct encounter with the Divine. This is called Sod ("mystery"), and refers to mystic or prophetic revelations and insights. When all four aspects of the study process are operating optimally, the student enters PaRDeS, "paradise."

Judaism and Christianity

I am including a short section on the relationship between Judaism and Christianity because I have found that what little is known about Judaism among many followers of Hinduism is strongly colored by the teachings of Christianity. Understanding Judaism through the lens of Christianity is like understanding Hinduism through the lens of Buddhism. The result is hampered, to say the least.

The analogy is more than apt. Just as Buddha was a Hindu, so Jesus was a Jew. Just as Buddha's parents were Hindus, so Mary and Joseph were Jews. Just as all of Buddha's Indian disciples were Hindus, so all of Jesus' apostles and the vast majority of his early followers were Jews. Just as the scriptures studied by the Buddha were Hindu Scriptures, so all the scriptures studied by Jesus were Jewish scriptures. Just as all of Buddha's teachers were Hindus, so all of Jesus' teachers were Jews. Just as Buddha became a *sannyasin*, so Jesus became a rabbi. And just as the teachings of Buddha were originally directed at Hindus, so the teachings of Jesus were originally directed at Jews. In fact it may be safe to say that prior to the creation of religions about Buddha and Jesus, both Buddha and Jesus operated effortlessly within the wide worlds of Hinduism and Judaism, respectively.

Let me lay out the four largest distinctions between Judaism

> "The original human diet as laid out in Genesis was strictly vegetarian. According to Torah, humans only began to eat animals after the Flood (Genesis chapters 6 through 9) when the earth was too wet to plant. Aptly, it is only then that animals are said to fear humans."

and Christianity. First, most Christians believe that Jesus was and is the Second Person of the Holy Trinity comprised of God the Father, the Son, and the Holy Spirit. Jews believe that Jesus was a rabbi and Jewish prophet, and no more or less divine than any other human being.

Second, while Christians believe that Jesus is the messiah ("anointed one") promised in the Hebrew Scriptures, Jews believe that the messiah has yet to arrive. Unlike the Christian idea of a heavenly messiah promising salvation in a heavenly realm, Jews await a fully human Messiah who will bring justice, compassion, and peace to this world.

Third, many but not all forms of Christianity believe in Original Sin, a state afflicting all humans that is passed on from one generation to another through procreation. According to the 4th century Church Father, St. Augustine, Original Sin leaves all humans utterly depraved, without the freedom to do good, and incapable of doing God's will without the help of God's grace. Judaism could not disagree more.

Judaism teaches that every person is born innocent rather than sinful, and that each one has the capacity to do good and evil as well as the ability to choose between them. In fact, from the Jewish point of view, part of spiritual practice as a Jew is to take ownership of the energies that could be used for evil and channel them to the good. Not only do we Jews believe humans have the capacity to do God's will, humans are given the ability to discern that will as well: whatever moves us toward justice, compassion, and peace, is the will of God, whatever does not, is not.

Fourth, while Christians may differ on the details, the general consensus among them is that hell is a place or state of suffering reserved for the unsaved — that is, those who do not accept Jesus Christ as their one and only Lord and Savior. Judaism could not be more different. Jews have no official position on the after–life, and speak very little of either heaven or hell, focusing instead on repairing the brokenness in this world (*tikkun ha–olam*) rather than worrying about our fate in the world to come. We believe that if there is a heaven, it is open to all who seek to do good in this world regardless of their faith or lack there of.

Conclusion

I would like to conclude this essay by offering a bit of guidance to those who may find yourselves working with Jews who come seeking a spiritual birth in other traditions.

First, please do not assume that they were taught any of the things that I have shared in this essay. Despite growing up in an observant Jewish home, I, myself, did not learn these things. My rabbis knew better than to try and impart authentic spiritual wisdom to a child. But when I was ready to learn, I had become so deaf to the deeper levels of my own religion that I assumed they did not exist. My experience is the norm. Most Jews do not know Judaism as a path of awakening.

Second, please do not send the Jewish seeker back to her or his rabbi. Few rabbis focus on Judaism as a path of awakening. Most are concerned with the communal aspects of Jewish life, with the fate of the State of Israel, and with issues of peace and justice in the political and social spheres, and not with God-realization. While the work of these rabbis is essential to the survival of our people, their strengths will not match the needs of the Jewish spiritual seeker, and sending the seeker "home" is only going to further his or her exile from Judaism and, perhaps, even from God.

Third, to help Jewish students understand the deepest levels of their root tradition, send them to rabbis who are steeped in these ideals and open to the questions of Jews who otherwise might never make their acquaintance. Or, if a Jewish seeker has no access to a rabbi in whom to confide, the Jewish seeker might be pointed towards the following books: *Everything is God* by Jay Michaelson (2009); *Seek My Face: A Jewish Mystical Theology* by Arthur Green (2003); *God is a Verb* by David Cooper (1998); or two of my own books *Open Secrets* (2004) and *Minyan* (1997).

Fourth, and finally, other religious traditions can take the Jewish seeker on as a student. This sharing of wisdom certainly does not confer any disrespect on Judaism with Jew. They only need to be taught that such wisdom can be found in Judaism as well.

Rabbi Rami Shapiro is an award-winning author, poet, essayist, and educator whose poems have been anthologized in over a dozen volumes, and whose prayers are used in prayer books around the world. Rami received rabbinical ordination from the Hebrew Union College–Jewish Institute of Religion and holds doctoral degrees in both Jewish studies and divinity. A congregational rabbi for 20 years, Rabbi Shapiro currently teaches Religious Studies at Middle Tennessee State University, and directs One River (**www.one-river.org**), a not-for-profit educational foundation devoted to building community through contemplative conversation. Rami writes a regular column for Spirituality and Health Magazine called Roadside Assistance on Your Spiritual Journey. His most recent books are The Sacred Art of Lovingkindness, The Divine Feminine, and Open Secrets from which this essay was adapted. Rabbi Rami can be reached through his website, **www.rabbirami.com**

◆ *Anam Thubten Rinpoche*

WITNESSING THE ECSTATIC DISSOLUTION OF THE SELF

This is a transcription of a dharma talk given by Anam Thubten Rinpoche on August 28th, 2006.

What is this spiritual realization that we often talk about? For example, someone has a realization, and then someone else has a smaller realization or a bigger realization, and so forth. What is this about? It is first about realizing what it is not instead of what it is. It is initially about realizing who we are not instead of who we are. It proceeds by realizing what we are not instead of what we are.

Who and What I am Not

And so, there comes a big opening in our spiritual understanding that realization is not about realizing who I am, or about rushing towards some distant destination that can be experienced if I realize who I am, like, I'm the mighty one, or I'm the whatever Buddha, or I'm the Vajrayogini, or I'm the Vajradhara, or my true essence is the same as theirs. There is almost a contest of racing toward that idealized spiritual destination.

And in the same way we tend to look up to those who may appear to be basically meeting our standard of what spiritual realization is. We have this very deep-seated tendency of trying to construct the ego's identity someway or another, and very subtly too. It's sneaky; it's not all that conscious sometimes. The ego is able to use us again and again, a sort of ignorant slavery, a mindless constructing of ego's indestructible castle — an indestructible castle of false identities.

This pure awareness that we're often speaking about is not really a state of "I know the truth," or "I have ownership of the truth so now I know who I actually am!" It's more about not finding even one speck of identity that we can call "This is who I am." It is losing all of our identities, rather like being left in the no-man's land. And what happens when we end up empty-handed like this, without having any identity, any illusion that we can hold onto as to who I am or what it is, without any place that we can look for refuge? What happens is very good to contemplate.

A State of Ecstatic Emptiness

There seems to be this prevailing notion among many spiritual seekers that the ultimate goal of the spiritual journey is to come to some kind of absolute realization of who we are. We want to know who we are, and we want to realize our true nature, but when we really get to the place where we no longer have any concepts, no longer have any fear, no longer have any doubt, then we come to a stark realization that actually we are nobody. We are no one, we are no thing.

Thus, Buddha-nature is not another state. Buddha-nature is not some kind of divine identity that we can hold onto, that nobody can take away from us. It is not like that. Buddha-nature is that consciousness wherein all identifications cease completely. We can call it buddha-nature, or luminous awareness, but it is that unique space where we are no longer operating our life from any egoistic viewpoint or particular framework of our mind. For, as long as we are still under this seductive influence of the ego, which is all about believing that we have to find ways to solidify our existence and then just keep constructing all these layers and ways of defending this flimsy egoic existence, we will never find true liberation.

Blessed Clarity and Vigil

So now we have to be very clear, a hundred per cent clear, without leaving any chance to be deceived again, without allowing the self to perpetuate its same old trends. We're now all about spiritual realization, and that is really about letting go of all our identities, all images, all self-images, completely. The ego will try and dictate to you, saying, "You cannot do that; if you do that the world is going to come to an end." To maintain its own separate existence, it will finally tell you that you can let go of everything, but you must keep at least one identity, the last identity, so you won't get lost in this gigantic universe, so that you won't get confused, or you won't become nothing. The ego does this to make sure you are safe, in case this whole idea of eradication of identity goes wrong. [laughter] It is "life insurance," in case this experiment of enlightenment is not going to work out for you, because there's no proof that it is going to. In truth, we don't know what is going to happen.

When you learn how to swim, the swimming instructor will tell you that you have to just relax, you have to let go of all fear. And there is a part of you that kind of believes that you have to let go of all your fear, resistance, etc., but it is difficult. It is the same with your life of practice. You want to relax, but you end up clenching your fist, or biting your lip. There's a part of you that believes that if you don't completely let go of your fear, resistance, and rather just hold on to at least one tiny itty-bitty piece of it in case what he (the teacher) is saying is not going to work out, then at least I will be saved. But this is not the case. The more you bite your lips, the more you try to make yourself stronger and put up resistance, the more you end up sinking into the water. What you really need to do is just relax completely, letting go of every form of resistance. Just relax and throw yourself into that ocean with complete trust and fearless awareness. Then you'll be fine. You'll be completely fine.

The Self-Surrender of Transparency

And that is what I am asking. That is what I'm asking of myself all the time, as well as of all of you, each and every moment. The assignment is very simple after all. The question is, "Can we let go of all our identities each and every moment?" This is a question that you really have to keep asking yourself. When you're meditating and when you are not meditating, when you are driving a car or when you are taking the teachings, or when you are that person putting gas into your tank, you always have to maintain this inquiry — this awareness that am I crazy enough to let go of all my identities without holding anything back. This can also be very subtle; it can be tricky. It requires a very sharp and keen awareness, even ruthless. Because, on one hand we may feel, "Oh I'm doing this extraordinary, exotic spiritual practice, or the *Dzogchen,* or the *Mahamudra,* and thereby eradicating my ego." But at the same time there's a part of you really racing and running towards gaining realization, of gaining a divine identity, and thereby not being able to really let go of all your false images, and attachment to all your self-images.

The ego's notion of who I am should go away completely from our consciousness, then. It's an intruder, after all, to the space of true awareness. The practice should proceed under the declaration, "I am not." I'm not buddha, I'm not ego, I'm not any false image I hold of myself. I'm not even my name, I'm not even my body, I'm not anything, basically. And in this practice, fear becomes the last stronghold of the ego. But in that moment when we just realize that fear is not who we are either, then there's immediate awakening, immediate realization. And that is the true realization we're talking about, wherein all our suffering goes away.

The Mafia Ego and its Henchmen

I always joke that ego is like the Mafia, the heartless Mafia. And fear, insecurity, hatred, jealousy — they're like the henchmen who are working for the ego boss day and night. You can't really get rid of the henchmen unless you get rid of the ego, the Mafia boss. You see? So you can try to get rid of jealousy, hatred, insecurity — try to get rid of all of them, but what about their source? And as a matter of fact, our life is pretty much consumed by really working and trying to transcend all these internal obscurations, especially those who are on the spiritual path who have been dedicating pretty much a huge portion of their lives to the practice of meditation, going to teachings, trying to transcend all these problems, trying to transcend the fact that they are unhappy, the fact that they are imperfect, the fact that they have all these spiritual and psychological problems like sadness, confusion, excruciating anguish. They tackle these through analysis, through doing all sort of methods. Obviously it's not working, right? In my case, it's not working. [laughter] So then, what should I do? Should I keep doing the same thing over and over? But then I would be fooling myself.

I think what happens along the way is that when we finally realize that nothing is working out, all the things we have done have not really uprooted our confusion, the inner samsara, so we finally say, "I give up on liberation. For all I know, it's just some kind of psychological solace." Well, doing spiritual practice and going to dharma teachings does provide us with some kind of psychological solace. And then we say, "Hallelujah! That's what I needed, and that's all I deserve. Liberation is not for me. It's for somebody else that's more brilliant than me." [laughter] Then you continue by thinking, "I used to be very brilliant. I used to care about liberation, awakening, but not anymore, because I just couldn't get it. I tried everything. I tried my principles, I tried my intelligence, I tried everything to get that so-called total awakening. It's not working, so finally I decided to be satisfied with having this periodic psychological solace." Right? And that kind of solace happens. Easily. It's not really that difficult to approach, just kind of beautiful, you know. Go to pujas, or do some meditation, light incense when I meditate, and just play some kind of nice fantasy in my head over and over again, such a fantasy as "I'm doing the right thing," or "I'm hanging around the right kind of people. My teacher is the best teacher, my sect is the most sublime sect," and so forth. So I'm doing the right thing.

That solace, that spiritual, psychological solace, is not total awakening, because it's impermanent and transient and we know inside that it doesn't last a long time. When we are forced to confront our personal challenges it doesn't really liberate you, it goes away, it disappears, and then we often discover ourselves as being in the middle of an internal hell, being beset by confusion, jealousy, hatred, judgment, dualism, and so forth. So that psychological solace is not really liberating us completely.

Dialogue with Truth

Now, what we really want is to have that complete, absolute, almost crazy, mad, passionate yearning for liberation more than anything else, and be ready to sacrifice that cherished psychological solace on behalf of the Great Awakening. Because the Truth tells you, "I will give you the liberation if you want, I will give you the awakening right now if you want — if that is really what you want." And as a matter of fact, the Truth has been knocking on your door from time immemorial, and you're the one who's pretending you didn't hear. Of course, it will not be given for free; you have to give up something. "What if I give a $10,000 check?" Truth will tell you, "No, that is not what I am asking for." "How about if I give you my house?" Truth will tell you, "No, that is not what I'm asking from you." "How about my freedom?" Truth says, "No." "How about my intelligence?" "No," comes back the answer.

And now you are running short of valuable things you can offer to get liberation. So you ask, "How about my absolute submission to you?" Truth says, "That's the last thing I want from you!" So then finally you say, "Truth, tell me, what do you want?" And Truth says, "I want your psychological solace. That's all you're holding onto. The fantasy about awakening, about enlightenment, that limited concept of the divine that you've been building on to — I want to take that solace away from you. It's going to hurt for a while, but it's going to be all right."

And once you accept that ultimate sacrifice, everything is fine. At such a moment, the ego disappears. The Mafia disappears into nothingness, into emptiness, along with all his vicious and wicked henchmen called hatred, jealousy, confusion, delusion. All of them disappears silently, without leaving even one single trace behind.

The Difficulty is in the Ego, Not the Practice

And this process doesn't have to be necessarily painful. I think sometimes that the way I present teachings can be a little bit dramatic. Over-dramatic, sometimes. It doesn't have to be a dramatic, painful, or impossible procedure — this assignment I'm speaking about right now — this whole work of letting go of all your identities, all of your images. It can be very blissful actually, sometimes. And that is what the path of the *Dakini*, or *Vajrayogini*, is all about. It's not all about going through unnecessary pain, or unnecessary austerity, or hardships in the course of letting go of all your fears, all your egoistic identities, in a single moment. That process can be done blissfully, ecstatically.

A few days ago, somebody asked me to write down a topic for a teaching I'm supposed to deliver sometime in the future, and as I went through the whole list of teachings I realized I have taught pretty much everything, or most of what I'm going to teach in the coming months. *Ngondro*, well, I'm teaching that sometimes — one can't really "teach" that. How about *Lojong*? Well, I tried that some time ago. How about Guru Yoga? I am about to teach that; it already appeared in my calendar, so I really can't pick up that topic soon. So finally I completely ran out of any material for teaching, as a topic. Then I sat and thought, and finally this phrase came to my mind — Witnessing the Ecstatic Dissolution of Self.

And that is what I'm really trying to speak about today. It can be titled "Witnessing that Ecstatic Dissolution of Self," but also the ecstatic death of the ego. I know that sometimes I talk as if I were reading a Shakespeare play, very dramatic, you know. "Sacrifice your blood" on behalf of finding awakening. [laughter] "End up disturbed in some sense," you know? But it can be very ecstatic. It can be very fun. It can be truly liberating.

Actually, sometimes even going into the possiblity of letting all of your identities go can be very liberating and blissful by itself. Of course, once you reach that awareness it would be truly amazing, in the way that even the great teachers speak about the bliss that comes out of realizing emptiness. It can never be expressed in words, it can never be measured, because it's the ultimate, the Supreme Bliss. It's the bliss of all blisses.

But even going into that place and thinking of the possiblity of transcending and giving up all these false identities, then there's always liberation too. It can be very beautiful when the ego begins to dissolve, because you realize that now you are finally dropping a huge burden, a rock or boulder that you've been carrying along through many lifetimes. Finally, you see it just slowly sliding off your shoulder and dropping to the ground. You realize that you didn't have to carry that boulder on your shoulder at all in the first place. There is a tremendous sense of freedom and joy, then, just watch that process of ego begin to dissolve into the Great *Sunyata*, Emptiness.

And at the same time you will be witnessing your fear, your anger, your hatred, all of them, begin to dissolve into nothingness. And emergence of awareness, compassion, and love begin to shine in your consciousness, as if you're watching a movie, as if you're watching a sunset, as if you're watching a very beautiful dance.

The Illusion of Suffering

Since we are very reward-and-goal-oriented creatures, we all want to know what I can get if I try and transcend all my identities. There actually is a reward, and that is to finally realize that suffering has never been existent in your life. The problem has never been existent in your life, and you must be awakened to this ever-excellent, all-perfect Reality. Suddenly, you transcend all your egoistic identities and realize the non-existence of your suffering, the non-existence of your problems. It is as if you have been living in the paradise, like *Akanishtha* — the land of bliss, Eternal.

And that's what we realize when the ego disappears, because the ego is very much the foundation and support for all these 84,000 kleshas. If we just try to transcend each of those 84,000 kleshas, the 84,000 mental defilements, it is like trying to avert a poisonous tree by cutting a few leaves and small branches off of it. They just grow back again, and the tree remains throughout.

So, the only way you can really completely eradicate that poisonous tree is to uproot it; take it away by the root. For, in the practice we have been applying most of the time, we are really trying just to fix the problems, a problem here and a problem there, and trying to work with our anger, our confusion, or trying to work with our depression, just trying to work with this and that but never really going to this deeper place in our consciousness where we can really remove all this by tackling the ego.

Ego's existence is very flimsy. It is fictitious; it is unreal. It is not like you have an assignment to take down a wall; that can be difficult, right? Because it is real. But the existence of ego in your consciousness is different, devoid of any real substance. Actually, you don't even destroy it. That's a mistaken concept. It is more that if you don't build the ego up, it soon disappears on its own. It's like fantasy.

Imagine that you have been having a really negative fantasy that keeps playing over and over in your consciousness. What will you do? Well, finally you realize this fantasy is destroying your life; it's eating away at your consciousness. If you try to destroy that fantasy, it only gets stronger, and stronger. What you need to do is just quit building and solidifying that fantasy. That fantasy disappears on its own, naturally, spontaneously, because it does not have any true concrete existence in and of itself. You only need to realize this.

In the same way, the ego does not have any solid concrete existence on its own. It is already practically bankrupt, but we foolishly run to it and provide it with a lot of funds and resources to maintain it. It's very expensive, too, and costs quite a lot. The cost is in freedom, peace, joy, and awakening. But somehow we feel that this expensive ego is who I am. We always declare,

"I am the ego, I am the self," so we end up dedicating a huge amount of personal expense to maintaining that existence.

It's like having an old beat-up car. When you have an old beat-up car, you pour money into its restoration. With all that financial output you could really buy a nice new car, but you have this old beat-up car. A lot of memories have happened in that car. You see? Maybe you found your first love in that car. So you just don't want to get rid of that car. It becomes some kind of a personal memory monument. It is quite expensive, because you will have to spend lots of money to repair and renovate it, and that car keeps breaking down constantly, but you feel that you have to always repair that car and drive that car because it is just your personal fantasy.

The Car Festival

In the same way, ego is like this car, a personal fantasy which is already falling apart from a long time ago, from time immemorial. It's flimsy. But we all feel that we really have to work hard for it, we have to dedicate all this energy to it, all this sacrifice to maintain it, because we believe it truly is who we are.

But it will be very amazing if any of us can try to Be, just Be without really having that sense of "I" or "me" or "mine." The ego constantly proposes, "Am I going to survive, am I educated or not, does the world revolve around me or not, do I have any place in this world or not?" You see? There is this habit of playing this self-indulgent game in our consciousness. It would be very nice to create a gap instead, where we just experience our Being without this constant need of identification with some form of identity. Even the idea of spiritual realization can work like that, to become the last basis of the ego's strategy for survival.

When I live fully, without this constant compulsive need to identify myself with a thing, or a thought, or an idea, or an illusion in my consciousness — what is that like? The flavor of just being? To simply allow yourself to feel that you're alive, that you're inhaling, and the air comes through your nostrils and fills up your lungs, and then goes away, and comes and goes away. That is a very freeing phenomenon, after all, even of itself.

What is it like, then, this momentary rest from always having to repair and maintain this old rusting piece of car-like ego? It is very beautiful, ecstatic too, even just witnessing the process. Ego just disappears. Let us say that you have this imagination of a demon who is always chasing after you, constantly annoying and bothering you, and never letting you sleep; always pursuing you. This demon or monster even has flames to burn you with. But then you get fed up and you start shouting at it, and you notice that this demon starts shrinking, just shrinking away, and you begin to see light everywhere. That is very beautiful, very ecstatic.

And once you know how to work this ecstatic process, this ecstatic dissolution of self, then you make contact with the eternal feast, the great celebration — the eternal celebration of bliss and awareness [happy laugh]. And every time the ego reappears, you can initiate, internally, that awareness, the ceremony of awareness, the witnessing of that ecstatic dissolution of the self! It's always ecstatic; it's the greatest celebration you can have, the greatest party you can have. Watching that dissolution of the ego is so much fun, is so ecstatic.

The Bliss of the Mahasiddhas

So I think that's why many of the Mahasiddhas speak about being completely blissed out each and every moment. These higher souls do not have to take hashish in India, you know! [laughter] They're constantly witnessing this beautiful divine dissolution, this ecstatic evaporation of the ego, and being charmed into forgetting all the problems of life because they're completely consumed and their consciousness is taken over by witnessing this beautiful ecstatic dissolution of the ego. And that becomes a constant state of mind.

So you see, life can be very fun if you allow yourself to just initiate that hidden eternal ceremony of witnessing the ecstatic dissolution of the ego. Then life becomes a great journey in a way that you never have to suffer any phenomenon or unsolvable problem from that moment on. Suffering can be completely ended, exhausted.

The question I want to ask right now is, Do you really believe that this is the truth? In order to believe, you have to try it, whether it works out or not. At least you have to try once, if not many times; at least you have to try witnessing that ecstatic dissolution of the problematic self. Whatever the outcome, it will be good for you to just try to go through that process of really living in the moment, a spacious moment in where you're no longer spending all this unnecessary energy to construct and reconstruct the illusory ego. You're simply just enjoying your own pure being, and seeing what that is like.

And truthfully, if you're completely residing in that realm of awareness where ego no longer is involved, then you realize what the truth is, you realize what the *Dharmakaya* is, and you realize what awakening is — right at that moment.

Anam Thubten grew up in Tibet and at an early age began to practice in the Nyingma tradition of Tibetan Buddhism. Among his many teachers, his most formative guides were Lama Tsurlo, Khenpo Chopel, and Lama Garwang. He is the founder and spiritual advisor of Dharmata Foundation, teaching widely in the U.S. and occasionally abroad. He is also the author of various articles and books in both the Tibetan and English language. His books in English include The Magic of Awareness, and No Self, No Problem.   website: www.dharmata.org

◆ *Swami Aseshananda*

REQUISITES TO SAMADHI
Only Renunciation is Fearless

Sri Ramakrishna, The Great Master, used to cite the saying which states, *"I would rather eat sugar than be sugar."* But on occasion He would also say about it, *"Few know the bliss of being sugar."* Philosophically speaking, the meaning is that most souls prefer form to Formlessness, but further, that few know or have ever had the experience of Formlessness, say, like Lord Buddha had, and came back to speak of it. *Savikalpa Samadhi* is experiencing God in form. *Nirvikalpa Samadhi* is nondual, the direct experience of God beyond all forms. Another possible interpretation might have it that "eating sugar" means experiencing all that the world of name and form has to offer, whereas "being sugar" translates as renouncing the world and seeking to establish oneself in oneness with Divine Reality — which is essentially formless.

There's a saying, "History repeats itself." Forty years ago I came to New York and New York greeted me with a terrific blizzard. A few people came by subway for Sunday lecture that day. The same thing happened today; the road is icy. What does it mean? It means that you have no control over nature. But you do have control over your reaction to nature.

Now, nature is the "steam" of the scientists. Scientists seek to control external nature. The Western civilization has achieved its glory, its power, and its grandeur on account of its scientific achievement, and in the face of many problems. In order to be successful in life you must "face the brute," as Swami Vivekananda used to say. Once he went to worship in the temple of Durga in Benares. Upon his return, a group of monkeys began chasing him. Then one holy man, one monk, yelled to him, *"Young monk, young sadhu, you'll be killed by these monkeys if you let them chase you. Turn and face the brutes!"* Later, Swamiji told us, *"I turned and faced the brutes, waved my hand and shook my staff at them, and all the monkeys fled."* Similarly, problems will come, and difficulties, but you have to face them in order to overcome them.

Greek Thought and Hebrew Thought

Now, the Western civilization is a dualistic civilization. Two important streams of thought have contributed to this beautiful civilization; this grand civilization; this wonderful civilization. These two streams of thought are known by the historians as Greek thought and Hebrew thought. Greek thought has given the Western civilization and culture its intellectualism, its reason. You must be a rational man. You must think out how to solve your problems. Plato and Aristotle are the important philosophers here. All the philosophers since Plato, in the Western world, have written footnotes to Plato.

And I liked Plato when I was a young student of Western philosophy. But later I changed my mind. It is Shankaracharya who appeals to me; Shankaracharya's nondual advaita. You see, Plato has posed dualism between subject and object. Then there is the monotheism that Hebrew thought has given. But ironically, monotheism also posits dualism between man and God.

Now we must look back and try to understand things. The philosophy of America is Aristotle's philosophy, because Aristotle is the father of the scientific method of the West — the analytical method. And Plato is the father of Idealism, Western Idealism. But both realism and idealism are just concepts. Shankara tells us to transcend realism and idealism and realize our true nature, which is infinite and not finite. But the Western man will not accept this. Meister Eckhart spoke about the real nature of man as uncreated essence, but the West rejected him.

It was Thomas Jefferson who gave the motivating power of living to America. Motivating power means "Life, liberty, and the pursuit of happiness." Jefferson was inspired by the rationalistic philosophers of Europe. He used the word rationalism. When he spoke of rationalism, it was the ghost of Aristotle who was speaking.

Power to Exercise the Path of Enjoyment

The recent editor of Prabuddha Bharata has written that Western scientists are seeking the God of Advaita. I do not agree. Western scientists are not seeking the God of Indian Advaita, they are seeking the God of intellectual conviction for purposes of bringing happiness to man through wealth, through power, through scientific achievement, and through an affluent society. In other words, Western man thinks in terms of social perfection. But when you are thinking of social perfection you will have to consider the individuals that make up society. And most individuals think in terms of *bhoga marga* — wealth, beauty, happiness, power — these things belong to the bhoga marga. What do we mean by the bhoga marga? That you attempt to idealize the real instead of striving to realize the Ideal. In other words, you think that the world is real. But Shankaracharya says no; the world is maya.

What is maya, then? This world has two facets. The first facet is called *nama rupa*, name and form. That is maya's doing. But the world in its essence is Spirit, is pure Consciousness. And you cannot realize pure Consciousness in the objective world unless you have realized pure Consciousness within the internal world. And that is the reason that Swamiji, in his beautiful message to America and to the West, quoted *"From dreams awake, from bonds be free."* Come to know your true nature to be disembodied, unfettered — the unbound Spirit. Your true nature is infinite. If Western man does not think like that, does not become intellectually convinced of that fact, then the West has not accepted Advaita. If the West accepts Advaita, then renunciation is a must. He must give up the path of enjoyment and follow the path of renunciation, like Christ did. What is meant by renunciation? The real meaning of it is deification.

Only the Illumined Soul Can Help the World

Every man, whether he is American or non-American, is a manifestation of the Divine Spirit. But he must come to recognize this, then realize it. But standing in the way there is this fundamental dualism between liberal and conservative. There is dualism between Catholicism and Protestantism. For a hundred years Catholics and Protestants fought in Europe. Religion has not brought peace; religion, on the other hand, has brought disharmony, fights, quarrels, misunderstandings, hate, war, and damaging rumors of war.

Who will solve this problem? Time magazine says that it will be "the work of the man of the year." This year he is a Russian, not an American [laughter]. But whatever the case may be, to really help the world we feel that he must be an illumined soul; he must be a universal man. He must think in terms of peace, of living a pure life with unselfish motives, and help bring these higher dreams of people to fruition.

This higher dream of mankind is not the world of hate and greed and pride, but the world of peace, harmony, joy, and faith in the divinity of the Soul. So in order to realize that dream one has to first think in terms of values. You may think that economic security, scientific achievement, and building an affluent society is the sole purpose of life, but when death comes you will not be able to confront it and say "Death, where is thy sting? Grave, where is thy victory?" In other words, you have not yet realized your true nature to be immortal.

And therefore, an illumined soul is one who, if an atom bomb or a hydrogen bomb falls before him, he will not be afraid. It reminds me of Alexander the Great and a monk of India who was his interpreter. Alexander was very happy with his interpreter, and wanted to bring him with him to Greece. The monk refused, so Alexander drew his sword and said, "Then I will kill you." The monk told him that this was the worst lie that he had ever heard in his whole life. "Who can kill me?" he retorted. "Fire cannot destroy me. Death cannot destroy me. I am the Atman, immortal!" And this is not just about Indian religion; this is also real Christianity.

Real Religion and the Merry-go-round of the World

Real Christianity is the realization of Atman and Brahman to be identical — "I and my Father are one." Christ spoke of this to his direct disciples, like Peter. It was Paul, however, that made Christianity a dogmatic Christianity. What do I mean by dogmatic Christianity? A Christianity of exclusiveness. It is Paul that introduced the theological concepts of original sin, of vicarious atonement, and that the Avatar comes only as a redeemer rather than an Exemplar.

Here in the West, for example, if you follow Paul, you really follow the second founder of Christianity. But Paul was not trained by Christ like Peter was. Paul was a contemporary of

> "Real Christianity is realization of the Atman and Brahman to be identical — 'I and my Father are one.' Christ spoke of this to his direct disciples, like Peter. It was Paul, however, that made Christianity a dogmatic Christianity. What do I mean by dogmatic Christianity? A Christianity of exclusiveness. It is Paul that introduced the theological concepts of original sin, of vicarious atonement, and that the Avatar comes only as a redeemer rather than an Exemplar."

Christ, but he was a Pharisee. And he persecuted the Christians. On the road to Damascus he was even an accomplice in Stephen's death. He held the cloak.

So I will not accept compromise to Christ's teachings. Once, Swami Vividishananda asked me why I was not going to the fun circus in the World's Fair? Swami Nityaswarupananda was going to be there, you see. Nityaswarupananda wanted to go to the fun circus, the ferris wheel. I said, "I have come out of the ferris wheel of the world, of the *samsara chakra*. Buddha used that word, the "wheel of samsara." I have come out of the wheel of samsara, I will not go back in." They said, "Then you hold our overcoats; that will do." [laughter] It reminds me of Paul, at that time Saul; he also held the cloak, like the overcoat. Then there was a little bit of heart searching and he heard a voice. "Saul, Saul, why doest thou persecute me?" And he was transformed at that instant. Okay, all well and good. But this does not mean that he attained Nirvikalpa Samadhi.

Swami Vivekananda came here to America, and when he went to Texas, one of the college students fired a gun behind him to shock him. Swamiji was unnerved, so they applauded him. Swamiji did not come to proselytize the Americans into Hinduism, you see; that is not the Vedantic way. Swamiji came to awaken the spiritual consciousness of the American people. Through America, then, the most powerful nation, it might go out to the rest of the Western world.

And so you find that this merry-go-round of happiness in the world will never bring fulfillment to any individual until he realizes his true Self. Not the apparent self; that belongs to time, that belongs to history — but the real Self, the Atman. People

> "People say that this is the age of the atom. I do not agree. This is not the age of the atom, it's the age of the Atman. If you really want to challenge the hydrogen bomb, or nuclear bomb, challenge it and its deluded makers through *Atmajnanam*, the inherent wisdom of the Soul that is within you."

say that this is the age of the atom. I do not agree. This is not the age of the atom, it's the age of the Atman. If you really want to challenge the hydrogen bomb, or nuclear bomb, challenge it and its deluded makers through *Atmajnanam*, the inherent wisdom of the Soul that is within you.

But this challenge must be made via your personal experience in a higher state of consciousness, in an exalted state of consciousness, you see. And that state of consciousness is called *Turiya*. Yesterday, we celebrated Swami Turiyananda's birthday. This fits very well, because he attained Nirvikalpa Samadhi, as well as Savikalpa Samadhi. In Savikalpa Samadhi he experienced the personal God, but in Nirvikalpa Samadhi he experienced the Impersonal. That is called supreme identity in the fourth state of Consciousness, called Turiya.

Five Famous Obstacles to Yoga

So in order to attain supreme identity, read the Chandogya Upanisad. There we find Narada. He was intellectually bright. He had tremendous power of reasoning. But he was not satisfied. He was thinking of this: what will happen to me in the future? Why does fear come on account of the unknown? Patanjali calls this *abhinivesa*, fear of death.

There are five obstacles for attaining spiritual enlightenment: *avidya, asmita, raga, dvesa,* and *abhinivesa*. If you read and study Indian philosophy, especially Vedanta philosophy, you will find that there is no such thing as sin. No original sin, not at all. But avidya is there. Avidya, forgetfulness of your true nature as Atman, has two powers that delude you: It hides the truth; and it distorts the truth. Thereby we forget that our real nature is infinite, and that this infinite Being is the real form of man.

If you seek, say, "Paradise Lost," to Vedanta that is due to your avidya, for paradise is a dream, just like this earth. On account of avidya, you see, we fall into the state of dreaming. And as long as dreams last, all our experiences seem to us to be real. This dream state, Shankara calls *maya*. When he is interpreting maya in this way, then he is talking of *Bhranti darshana* — not seeing things in their own real light.

Avarana shakti is maya's power to cover truth, like a cloud covers the sun. Today, the sun is hidden, and therefore you think the sun has gone. No, the sun has not gone out. Take a helicopter or a mono plane and go above the clouds, or go to California, and you will find a beautiful sunset. Once I was traveling from Portland to Medford, and there was nothing but rain, rain, rain. We crossed the border into California and there was a beautiful sunset over Mt. Shasta. The sun never loses its power of shining. Similarly, the Atman, the real Self of man, never loses the power of knowing, its power of living, its power of Bliss — Satchitananda. In contrast to this Bliss you have hypnotized yourself into thinking, "I am happy with this world. I live in an affluent society. I live in a blue ribbon district." But one transcends ephemeral happiness, desire for affluence, and blue ribbon pleasures in Atmic realization.

Real happiness will come only when you discover your true nature. In order to discover your true nature, you have to live a pure life. You have to live a silent life, a holy life. A life based on dharma, based on building character so that you can live in the unimpeachable, spotless, and stainless Self.

Purification of Mind Leading to Freedom in Life

Spiritual life and it successful practice is like housekeeping. There is a first floor, there is a basement, and a second floor. Now, what do you do with all your unwanted things when it comes time to create space? Do you just put all your things that are unwanted in the basement? That will not really do the job. Those unwanted things, you should burn them. Similarly, in spiritual life, you must burn via the method of renunciation. It comes down to the burning of *samskaras* — those old unwanted remnants of thought patterns. Then create new samskaras for the first and second floor.

It is through the company of illumined souls we can get new samskaras. Then, when the samskaras are pure, when your thoughts are pure, then your mind stuff, *chitta*, will be pure. When the mind stuff is pure, then there will be constant and unbroken remembrance of God. When we use the word "mind stuff," it refers to samskaras, or mental impressions. Samskaras build the character of the individual. And unless one's character is stainless it will not be possible to realize God, because God vision or realization is a transcendental state of consciousness. It is a superconscious experience.

And therefore, one has to first purify the samskaras by living an ethical life. One also must control the emotional nature of the mind. Out-of-control emotions are the unnecessary clutter in the basement of the ego. So. self-mastery is necessary. As the Upanisads tell us, you see, the senses are the horses, while mind stands for their reins. And one's discriminating intelligence is the charioteer. When the mind has a good charioteer who knows how to control the horses by firm determination and an iron will, then these reins become firm, strong, and stable. Then he will reach the great goal. That means he will reach perfection, reach *jivanmukti*.

Freedom from the Senses, Not Freedom to the Senses

What we want, then, is freedom from the senses, not freedom to the senses, for the latter will create bondage. Freedom from the senses creates enlightenment — freedom from the tyranny of old age, disease, and death. And that is the reason why the disciples of Sri Ramakrishna, especially Swami Turiyananda, were not afraid of death.

Once, a CID officer wanted to test him, and became his devotee. He would bring the swami fruits. He would listen to his lectures with great attention. Later, he revealed himself and said, "I have been authorized to come here by the higher authorities. Are you not afraid?" "Why should I be afraid of you?" Turiyananda replied, "I am not even afraid of death! Besides, I've not done anything wrong." And so the swami silenced him. He was like a lion. A serpent once crawled on his body, but he did not do anything. "How did you feel?" he was asked. "Were you not afraid?" "Why?" he said. "If I was attached to the body, then there would have been fear, but I am not attached to the body; I'm attached to the Spirit."

My point is that great strength is necessary. And real strength comes from realization, realization of the truth which will make you free. If you attach to your apparent self, your happiness will be momentary. And that is the reason why I can say that Advaita Vedanta brings us good news. Why? Because it tells you that your real nature is infinite, that by knowing your real nature you will be immortal — *ananda rupam amritam*. You have to realize this in meditation. First, you get intellectual conviction, then you practice attainment of virtues. Next comes meditation, when your mind is concentrated. Finally, in a deep concentrated state of mind, the distinction between subject and object will disappear. A musician is one with his music. A dancer will be one with her dancing. A poet will be one with his poem. Similarly, a lover of God will be one with his beloved Lord. You may respond that there will be a distinction between lover and beloved. But Advaita philosophy states, not in the highest realization. And that is the reason why Swami Vivekananda sometimes quoted from Sufism.

The Secret of Real Love

A sufi mystic once knocked on the door of his beloved. A voice inside asked, "Who are you?" He mentioned his name. But the door remained closed. The second time he knocked and he mentioned his name, the door also remained closed. Then, the third time, he responded, "I am myself, my beloved." Then the voice said, "There is only space for one in here, not for two." The meaning of this story is that in real love there will not be any distinction between the individual soul and the universal soul. Love, lover, and beloved, will be one.

Real happiness will come when you have that rare type of love. Eros type of love remains selfish. Philias type of love will be philanthropic, based on humanitarian goodwill. But real love, transcendental love, is loving the Divine within and without. Although this distinction of within and without is created by the intellect, in real experience it will disappear.

> "First, you get intellectual conviction, then you practice attainment of virtues. Next comes meditation, when your mind is concentrated. Finally, in a deep concentrated state of mind, the distinction between subject and object will disappear."

Sri Ramakrishna Guru Deva Samprite

Sri Ramakrishna sometimes cited this distinction using the metaphor of tasting sugar and being sugar. When the distinction is there, that will be called Savikalpa Samadhi. That is penultimate samadhi. It is likened to Christ saying, "*I am the vine and you are the branches.*" But in Nirvikalpa Samadhi, this distinction will disappear. The teaching of *bheda*, whether they are called *sagata bheda*, or *svajatiya bheda*, or *vijatiya bheda*, all kinds of bhedas, distinctions, will disappear. Then there will be only the Supreme Identity. Examples of this are Sanat-kumara and Sukadeva, who followed the *jnana marga/vichara marga* and realized Nirvikalpa Samadhi. In our own modern times, Sri Ramakrishna realized Nirvikalpa Samadhi. He is the symbol of Advaita jnan — knowledge of nondual experience of God. Holy Mother is the symbol of the dynamic aspect of Brahman.

Sri Ramakrishna explained both Saguna Brahman and Nirguna Brahman from his own personal experience. This makes Him the ideal spiritual teacher whose message is a message of Enlightenment. The difference between Sri Ramakrishna and Shankara, then, would be that Sri Ramakrishna was not satisfied with jivanmukti alone. Sri Ramakrishna wanted his disciples to think in terms of *Sarvamukti* — freedom for all. That is why Swami Turiyananda, often quoted, "*Brahman satya, jagad mithya — Brahman is real, world is unreal.*" That statement is for the sadhaka. But for an illumined soul, the saying is "*Brahman satya, jagad satya — Brahman is real, world is also real.*" For them, the world is a manifestation of the Divine Mother. Life, as well as death — both are symbols and expressions of Mother Divine. There is a beautiful line in one of the poems of Swamiji that states: "*The shade of death, and immortality, both these, O Mother, are thy grace. May thy gracious face never turn away from me, thy child.*"

Grace and Self-effort, Hand in Hand

Sri Ramakrishna talked not only of self-effort, but also of Divine Grace. Buddhism speaks mainly of self-effort, as in "*Be a lamp unto yourself.*" Christianity speaks mainly of Divine Grace as well, as in "*....to thy hand I commend myself.*" But in this age, Sri Ramakrishna has built a bridge between self-effort and Divine Grace. When he says, "*Be like a good sailor and raise your sails on the mast of your sailing ship,*" that means that you must perform sadhana to realize God. But eventually you will realize that through sadhana alone you cannot realize Him. You can realize Him only through His Grace. And that is called the "Ascent of man." It is for the purification of the heart. But realization of God is due to Grace — the descent of God in the form of Grace. When that Grace of God comes to man, he realizes his true nature to be *nitya shuddha buddha mukta* — eternal, enlightened, ever free, never bound, immortal, and deathless.

So, real happiness only comes through the realization of God. And man can only give happiness to others when he has found happiness within himself. You cannot really help other people unless you have become an illumined soul. Those great illumined souls who are called the direct disciples of the Master are the source of our inspiration, the fountainhead of our joy, and also the spring of our inspiration.

I had the good fortune to serve one of the Master's direct disciples. I even slept at the feet of Swami Saradananda. And I can give testament to the fact that Swami Saradananda has never left me all these years. Residing in this country for 40 years, I have lived because of the memory of Swami Saradananda; he has given me great strength, has given me encouragement, has given me the inspiration to live an exemplary life and to give my message with confidence and with fearlessness. May this very fearlessness spring forth in your heart too, and make you strong.

Swami Aseshananda, a direct disciple of Sri Sarada Devi, Sri Ramakrishna's wife and spiritual consort, was the Spiritual Minister of the Vedanta Society of Portland for over forty years. He also received holy company with some of the direct disciples of the Great Master. He is the author of Glimpses of a Great Soul, on the life and teachings of Swami Saradananda.

Only Renunciation is Fearless

Five select verses from Bhartrihari's famous Vairagya Shatakam

Arise! Let us go into the forest
Where pure roots and fruits will be our food,
Pure water our only drink, pure leaves our bed,
And where the mean-minded, the thoughtless,
And those whose hearts are cramped with wealth
do not exist.

What if you own wealth that fulfils every desire?
What if your foot rests on the heads of your foes,
What of that?
What if you have made all your love wealthy,
If your body remains a Kalpa — what of that?
The only thing to be desired is Renunciation
Which gives all love to Shiva — For....

In enjoyment is the fear of disease;
In high birth, the fear of losing caste;
In wealth, the fear of tyrants;
In honor, the fear of losing her;
In strength, the fear of enemies;
In beauty, the fear of aging
In knowledge, the fear of defeat;
In virtue, the fear of scandal;
In the body, the fear of death.
In this life, all is fraught with fear.
Renunciation alone is fearless

So fear only life that brings birth and death.
Have no love of friends, no lust, no attachment.
Alone, living in seclusion in a forest,
What more is to be longed for than
Renunciation.

Oh mother earth, father wind,
Friend light, sweetheart water,
Brother sky, here,
take my last salutation with folded hands!
For today I am melting away into Brahman.
My heart became pure and all delusion vanished
Through the power of Renunciation.

Translation: Swami Vivekananda

Abbot Kyogen Carlson ♦

BIRTH, DEATH, & THE BARDO PLANE

This edited transcription of Kyogen's talk, transcribed by Jeff Stookey and edited by Genko Rainwater, was offered on June 15, 2014. Kyogen left the body suddenly on September 18, 2014. SRV Associations includes this engaging article on the bardo states in this edition of Nectar in honor and memory of his exemplary life.

It is wonderful to see everyone here after our recent move to this new location. I meant to say that at breakfast, too. We were all there…the same teapot, the same bowls, and the same wonderful people. Oh, we're all still here. So thank you all for making this transition happen so nicely.

Today's talk is entitled "Birth, Death, and the Bardo Plane." This week's bulletin had a description of the fact that we'd left the Madison Street place and were starting this place, and we had a matriculation ceremony [high school seniors from Dharma School to the adult Sangha] and I thought, "Well, there you are: 'Birth, Death, and the Bardo Plane,' and you can figure out which is which."

Birth and Death. These are concepts that we know. Any adult knows what birth and death is. We all experience them all around us. We see them happen. One thing that's true is that nobody really understands them. We see them, we know what they are, but nobody really understands. It's a mystery. In addition, Buddhism and Zen have a particular understanding of it. I'll get to that a little later.

Defining the Bardo

The *Bardo* plane, however, is even more mysterious. "Plane" here means a realm or a state. Bardo is a Tibetan word. It is now commonly used in American Buddhism. One thing I like about American Buddhism is that it has taken terms, expressions, and practices from all the different traditions, so all the different lineages refer to Bardo, even though it's a Tibetan term, and most lineages use words like *Sanzen* and *Zafu*, which is Japanese, and most also use the term *Metta* which is Pali, from Southeast Asia. Bardo is a Tibetan translation of the Sanskrit word *Antarabhava*. That's the original, Antarabhava, and it means "in-between state."

So look around. Our old life, our old venue, is gone; our new life, our new venue, is now under construction. So that's death and birth, and here we are in the Bardo plane — in-between. If you look on the wall over here, there's a big leopard [a mural of the Jason Lee Leopards]. One of the things about the Bardo Plane in the way that it is often described, is that there is a phase when wild beasts start nipping at your heels to propel you on, you know, to get you moving. So we're well afoot.

I'm going to give a little historical information about how the antarabhava, the Bardo, the in-between state, has been viewed. It's got a long history. I'm drawing here from Wikipedia:

"Used loosely, the term 'Bardo' refers to the state of existence intermediate between two lives on earth. According to Tibetan tradition, after death and before one's next birth, when one's consciousness is not connected with a physical body, one experiences a variety of phenomena. These usually follow a particular sequence of degeneration from, just after death, the clearest experiences of reality of which one is spiritually capable…."

This is that letting go we hear about. The end of something. There's a cessation. We talk about the first pure precept of cessation [Cease from Evil, Release All Self-Attachment]. That's complete cessation. So there's a moment of real clarity there.

"…and then proceeding to terrifying hallucinations that arise from the impulses of one's previous unskillful actions." Now this sequence is significant, and I'll come back to that.

For the prepared and appropriately trained individuals, the Bardo offers a state of great opportunity for liberation, since transcendental insight may arise with the direct experience of reality, while for others it can become a place of danger as the karmically created hallucinations can impel one into a less than desirable rebirth.

That is how the Bardo Plane is generally understood. I should mention that the Tibetan Buddhist view of the Bardo is very elaborate and is built up over time. But much earlier in India, different Buddhist schools debated this concept of intermediate existence, so that the *Sarvastivadans* and four other major schools accepted this intermediate state, while the *Theravadins* and the *Mahasamghikas* did not. But it is upheld in Vasubandu's *Abhidharma Kosha*.

This what Wikipedia states, quoting Fremantle:

"Originally, bardo only referred to the period between one life and the next. And this is still its normal meaning when it is mentioned without any qualification. There was considerable dispute over this theory during the early centuries of Buddhism, with one side arguing that rebirth (or conception) follows immediately after death, and the other saying that there must be an interval between the two. With the rise of Mahayana, belief in a transitional period prevailed. Later Buddhism [particularly Tantric and Tibetan] expanded the whole concept to distinguish six or more similar states [bardo states], covering the whole cycle of life, death, and rebirth. But it can also be interpreted as any transitional experience, any state that lies between two other states. Its original meaning, the experience of being between death and rebirth, is the prototype of the bardo experience, while the six traditional bardos show how the essential qualities of that experience are also present in other transitional periods."

So by this teaching, it's right here. It's right here!

By refining even further the understanding of the essence of bardo, it can then be applied to every moment of existence. The present moment, the now, is a continual bardo, always suspended between the past and the future. This is close to a Zen perspective, although Zen says "let's not get so complicated about this – life is flow. That's it."

The Classic Bardo Experience

Here's a quick description of the classical Bardo experience. At the moment of death there is a radiant light that appears. It's like this tunnel, this white light, and this goes back to early Buddhist teachings. There's this radiant light that is a portal directly into nirvana. If we can let go and move forward completely, completely, at that moment, we can enter. However, karma and habit energy make it difficult. So it means that you have to be well prepared, have already dropped a lot of baggage. If you're hauling a lot of baggage you just can't get through that portal. So we slip past.

At this juncture some very beneficent beings come forward, very gentle and loving beings, and try to encourage us into beneficial rebirth. But again, if karma and habit energy make it difficult to accept this offering, we slip past. So working on our karmic entanglements in this lifetime is really important for making this transition work smoothly.

This slipping past the mark continues like this until we get to what may be called "the wild beast stage," a kind of ripping and clawing in us which propels us into rebirth on base desire. And so we find parents that match our karma and, voila!, conception — and where karma leads us. We're sort of whipped around by karma, instead of directing ourselves in a more conscious way.

Life in the Bardo, and Benign Entities

Here are some everyday life versions of Bardo, and what life and death, or birth and death in a general Buddhist sense, is. For example, the loss of a relationship, that's a death of a self. The self that is in a relationship that is disintegrating, feels this loss of self as the relationship disintegrates over time. The loss of a job also does that, as well as any kind of loss where there's an entanglement with any condition that is just deteriorating.

In Zen terms, death is every moment, every moment a self dies. Birth is every moment a self appears. Letting go of one moment and stepping into the next is life and death. Birth and Death. So it's a dramatic change we feel at the loss of a self that's wrapped up with a circumstance or a condition. That is why I use this example of someone habitually bound into bad relationships. That's a habit pattern, a habit energy that's very difficult to break. When someone who does this is coming to the end of a bad relationship, that's a death, and it's traumatic and difficult, dramatic, and eventually the relationship dissolves.

But importantly, in those pivitol moments there is also the light of liberation which is available if we want to walk towards it. But karma and habit energy make it very difficult. We can feel a certain liberation there, but we are dragging all this baggage along so we don't really take the steps that we should.

It is then that these beneficent beings come forward — all their friends, all the people who commiserate — and offer advice. They say, "Why don't you do something different this time?" And, "I know a nice guy." And, "Here's a nice birth, try this one." But habit energy is really strong, and people are inclined to go back to only what they know. So they don't take these suggestions; and maybe they are not so good anyway, but they have an opportunity to do something different, and they don't.

In worse case scenarios, eventually things get worse, and get more difficult, and these beings stop coming around, stop being so kind, and pretty soon this compulsion towards rebirth appears. People want to repeat this rebirth of the self in relationship. This is a strong impulse, karma and habit energy, so they look for someone who matches their previous incarnation, and they fall into that same pattern again. That's a general description of the Bardo Plane, and how karma and habit energy work in this transition we call Bardo, or intermediate state.

An important point here is that beings can move on at any point in the transitional period, and sooner is better than later. There's more liberation there, although some people can choose to make a bad decision just like that [snap], so that's not always the case. But as far as in terms of this Bardo description, when we take the options quickly, we're more likely to make good choices.

Zen and Bardo

Our Zen tradition doesn't go into a whole lot of discussion about this sort of thing; it's more simple. Daily life practices die completely each moment. Say "Yes." If something falls apart, don't hesitate, just say "Okay, it's gone." Be born without hesitation. Say "Yes." But always with open hands. This is immediate transition without an intermediate state. The kind of birth and death I'm talking about here is in every affirmation that we experience, every success, every word of praise, there is the birth of a self. We receive it. Sometimes it's very difficult to receive this praise or this affirmation. Zen says receive it completely, but with open hands. No attachment. It's just what it is. Sometimes we're very busy trying not to notice this affirmation. We should notice it. Appreciate it. But not be caught in it.

Every negation, every word of blame, every failure is a death. Every loss is a death of a self. Our expectation, our hope is dashed, and there's a self bound up in it that's gone. Accept it completely. No resistance. But no regret either. You know, just "let it be."

And what we do with these two things, birth and death, affirmation and negation, even as we accept it, is still up to us. We choose how we respond, we just have to accept that it is. And it's not fatalism. It's just what it is, and we respond to it as whole-heartedly as we know how. Wisdom arises from this. We let both come, we let both go. Each moment is new, but we need to be clear of exactly what each moment brings, what the truth of it is. Then we can take the best action within that state. Resisting one and grasping the other is just like the Bardo Plane — we don't move on to the next clear moment, but stay in this resistant stage fighting it, in this "if-only" stage of all that stuff.

So we are dragged by our stubbornness into whatever comes next instead of choosing.

Looked at this way, this room, this moment in the flow of Dharma Rain is not a Bardo Realm at all; it is our next rebirth. This is it. Here we are, if and when we fully embrace it, and we're doing really well. I appreciate that.

You can think of this as positive thinking without expectation. It is different from wishful thinking, being positive to try to get what you want. The power of positive thinking is close, but "no cigar." There's birth attachment, or death aversion, in trying to manipulate circumstances by being real positive about them. That kind of works; I mean, if you're really positive, good things tend to happen. But if you are open-handed you can actually see what is present much better, can see the opportunities that are really there. If you have your eye on a particular thing, you can miss what's there, trying to get something else. Just be positive. Just say yes, but without attachment.

So, practice leads to a balance of birth and death, joy and disappointment, and this is liberation.

The Koan of Chinese Ch'an Master, Baizhong

Here's a koan, the famous Baizhong's fox, which is Case 8 in the *Book of Serenity*. Also Case 2 of *The Gateless Gate*.

Baizhong is a famous Chinese Ch'an master [Zen master] in the Tang dynasty, in the classical period. He established the monastic rules, and his temple is venerated for that because it freed the Ch'an tradition from Imperial and noble interference and allowed it to become more independent.

The story is, that for a period of time he gave his morning talk to the assembly, and he would notice that there was an old monk at the back of the assembly whom he didn't recognize. The old monk turned up every morning for a period of time and then as the assembly broke up, he disappeared and was just gone.

But one morning after the assembly dispersed, he was still there. And he came forward to Baizhong and he said, "I have a question. In an age in the past I was the priest of this mountain [mountain is often used as a term for a temple]. While I was the priest here, a monk asked me: 'Is an enlightened person bound by cause and effect, bound by karma?' and I answered 'No.' We can free ourselves from our karmic entanglements, but when he asked this question 'is he still bound by karma?' I said no, and because of this answer I have been born as a wild fox over and over for 500 years. I've been listening to your teaching and I hope you can speak the turning word for me and liberate me."

And Baizhong said, "Ask me that question." And the old monk said, "Master, is the enlightened person bound by karma, or not?" And Baizhong said, "The enlightened person is not deceived by karma."

And at that moment he was awakened, and he told Baizhong, "I'm not really a monk now at all, I'm the ghost of a dead fox, and you'll find my body on the other side of the mountain in a cave. Please give me the burial of a monk." And so the next day, Baizhong had the monks go out into this particular place where they found the fox, and they gave him this funeral of a monk inside that fox cave. We actually saw that cave on a pilgrimage there in 2012.

I use this story a lot with people. Do not be deceived by karma, just see it clearly, understand it. That's the first step. Sometimes in the story, instead of him saying, "not being deceived by," it's translated as "do not be blind to," or "karma is not obscured to an enlightened being."

Here is some of the commentary on this koan in the *Book of Serenity*:

"On Baizhong Mountain in Hong prefecture, every time Ch'an master DaiJi [an honorific title for Baizhong] ascended the high seat, there was always an old man listening to his teaching. The old man had dwelt on this mountain in the time of Kashapa Buddha. Because he had answered a student mistakenly, up to the present he had degenerated into a wild fox being. Indeed, it was because he himself leaned on a fence and stuck to a wall, sending people off to fall into a pit or plunge into a ditch."

That means grasping, grasping attached to purity and to his own answers.

"Baizhong, however, based his answer on actuality rather than falling into cause and effect, a forced denial, or a nihilistic view. Not being blind to cause and effect, his findings were wondrous and in step with the flow. Here, causality is accepted, and there is a natural and even flow with it."

Causality is present. We flow with it. Not being blind to cause and effect is finding the wondrous along with the flow.

"Have you not heard it told, how when Ch'an Master Juan was in the assembly of Ch'an Master Wei, he heard two monks bring up this story. One monk said, 'Even if he is not blind to cause and effect, he still hasn't shed the wild fox body.'"

This means he has to stop being a wild fox. He has to act otherwise in order to be born otherwise. You can accept truth, but you've got to take that step to realize it. Step into the rebirth.

"The other monk replied, 'Just this, is not falling into cause and effect, for when has he ever fallen into cause and effect?'"

Now this means that having the body of a wild fox is not the problem. Being stuck to it is. Being trapped in it is.

"The master was startled and considered these words unusual. He then hurried to the bamboo cluster hermitage on Mt. Huangbo. As he crossed a valley stream he was suddenly enlightened. He saw Master Nan and told him what had happened. Before he finished, tears were streaming over his jaws. Master Nan made him sleep soundly on the attendant's bench. But suddenly he got up and wrote a verse:

> Not falling, not blind,
> for monks or lay folk there are no taboos.
> The bearing of a free man is like a king's.

> How can he accept the enclosure of a bag
> or covering by lid?
> One staff can be horizontal or vertical.
> The wild fox leaps
> into the company of the golden lion.

"Not falling, not blind," and therefore not deceived. "For monks or lay folks there are no taboos" means no traps, no snares.

"The bearing of a freeman is like a king's" means liberation is nobility.

"How can he accept the enclosure of a bag or covering by lid?" means no labels, no roles. It's not about that.

"One staff can be horizontal or vertical" means high and low is of no concern. the fox body is of no concern.

"The wild fox leaps into the company of the golden lion" infers that the golden lion is an epithet of the Buddha.

At this level of practice we are to hold no distinction between ordinary beings and sages, make no distinction between foxes and lions. We do not become trapped.

Reflections

So think back to the Bardo story of bad relationships, five hundred years of bad relationships. Oy! I think that's far worse than a fox. Being stuck over and over is like Groundhog Day. This is a Bardo Plane. Our practice is to let go completely. No avoiding death. Step forward completely without hesitation. Embracing birth. No resistance. No Bardo.

So it occurs to me about this argument early on in India, is there a transitional stage or not? Both sides are right. Done really well with no grasping or aversion, there is no intermediate state. Moment [snap]. Moment [snap]. Moment [snap].

What is grasping and aversion Bardo? And just so, any relationship could be fine. This person in a bad relationship stepping out of their own role may find they can be in it. You understand? They may be able to be in that relationship just fine. That is rare, but it's possible, if one has the bearing of liberation within.

The last word goes to Dogen. This is from *Shushogi*:

"The thorough clarification of the meaning of birth and death is the most important problem for all Buddhists. Since the Buddha dwells within birth and death, enlightenment exists within birth and death. The latter do not exist. Simply understand that birth and death are in themselves nirvana, there being no birth/death to be hated, nor nirvana to be desired. Then, for the first time, you will be freed from birth and death. Realize that this problem is of supreme importance."

> Just this.
> It is not about concepts or abstractions;
> it is about practice.
> Each day, each moment,
> non-opposition to the flow of change,
> to what we like and what we do not like,
> clinging to neither, resisting neither,
> but also, whole-heartedly stepping into each moment
> — that is the practice that defies birth and death.
> Then birth and death are nirvana itself.
> And this very hall is already the Buddha realm. ~ ~ ~
> Abbot Kyogen Carlson

The late Kyogen Carlson was abbot and godo of the Dharma Rain Zen Center in Portland, Oregon, up until his recent passing in September of 2014. As an author, his books include Zen in the American Grain, and Discovering the Teachings at Home.   www.dharma-rain.org

TIBETAN BUDDHIST BARDO BY JAMGON KONTRUL RINPOCHE

Chart by Babaji Bob Kindler, Courtesy of SRV Association

 ## Teachings on Bardo States

() The Bardo of Death and Rebirth ()

"This teaching is extraordinarily important for our present day world, because today we live with widespread conditions of distraction that weaken our ability to concentrate fully upon whatever practice we are engaged in."

Jamgon Kongtrul Rinpoche

TATHAGATAGARBHA — Buddha Nature

"Tathagatagarbha pervades all beings in quantity as well as in quality. It is primordial Essence which is never defiled. It becomes obscured, however, when an individual engages in negative activity and thus accumulates karma which prevents recognition of It."

"Only with fearlessness can we maintain mindfulness and awareness, free from distraction."
Jamgon Kongtrul Rinpoche

A duration of some 7 days ———

The Intermediate State Between Death & Rebirth }

"....an excellent time to realize Buddha Nature...."

A duration of some 14 days ———

A duration of some 28 days ———

The Three Phases of the Bardo Between Death and Rebirth

"All three of these phases offer an opportunity to recognize the nature of mind and attain enlightenment."

1) The Bardo of the Moment of Death

a. Earth dissolving into Water ———→
   External Sign — Weakness
   Internal Sign — Foggy Perception

b. Water dissolving into Fire ———→
   External Sign — Dryness of mouth, eyes.
   Internal Sign — Dreamlike Experiences

c. Fire dissolving into Air ———→
   External Sign — Loss of warmth
   Internal Sign — Consciousness is unstable

d. Air dissolving into Consciousness →
   External Sign — Exhalation; no inhalation
   Internal Sign — Awareness is a steady light

2) The Bardo of Buddha Nature ———→
   Lights of five colors appear, associated with the five Buddhakalas and various deities.

3) The Bardo of Becoming ———→
   Lights of lesser intensities appear, associated with the six modes of existence, and one relives the deeds of the past life.

"Those lacking training may panic here. It is important to understand that awareness is not changing, only the elements are dissolving."

"All experiences become like mirages, and moving images take on a dreamlike nature."

"Consciousness appears like a flame, but it is unsteady due to constant movement."

"Awareness becomes like a lamp that is no longer disturbed by wind."

"Deities emanating through mandalas appear in peaceful and wrathful aspects representing emptiness or clarity."

"If a man fails to recognize Buddha nature then he is prepared to be reborn in one of the six realms of rebirth."

"If you practice hard enough, you can gain enlightenment in this life, and that is best. If your practice in this life was guided by a spiritual teacher, then you will experience the clear light at the time of death and recognize the nature of mind. If that does not happen, there is a possibility to do so after death. There are practices one can do at the time of death. A spiritual master can also introduce the dying person to the bardo in such a way that he or she will recognize the clear light when it occurs."

Jamgon Kongtrul Rinpoche

SRV Associations — Babaji's Teaching Schedule, 2015

SRV Hawai'i
Administrative Office
PO Box 1364
Honoka'a, HI 96727

SRV Associations'
website: www.srv.org
email: srvinfo@srv.org
Phone: 808-990-3354

SRV Oregon
1922 SE 42nd Ave.,
Portland, OR 97215
Ph: 503-774-2410

SRV San Francisco
465 Brussels Street
San Francisco, CA 94134
Ph: 415-468-4680

February/March, 2015

SRV San Francisco (Meditation, 6 to 7 am)
2/13 Fri   7:00pm Arati/Satsang with Babaji
2/14 Sat   9:30am Class: Upanisads
           7:00pm **Sri Ramakrishna Birth Puja**
2/15 Sun   9:30am Class: Upanisads

SRV Oregon (Call for meditation times)
2/20 Fri   7:00 pm Satsang with Babaji
2/21 Sat   9:30am Class: Upanisads
           6:00pm **Sri Ramakrishna Birth Puja**
2/22 Sun   9:30am Class: Upanisads
2/25 Wed   7:00pm Vedanta 101, with Annapurna Sarada
2/26 - 3/2 — SRV Winter Retreat

SRV Winter Retreat, 2/26 - 3/2, Seattle, Wa.
Subject: Panchadasi & Panchakarana
(arrive Thursday night)
For more information call SRV Office, 808-990-3354

3/4 Wed 7:00pm Principles of the Upanisads, with Anurag

3/7-8 – Short Weekend Seminar
Subject: How a Householder Renounces the World
2 classes Saturday, & 1 class Sunday morning

May, 2015

SRV San Francisco (Meditation, 6 to 7 am)
5/1 Fri   7:00pm Arati/Satsang
5/2 Sat   9:30am Class: Shankara & the Upanisads
           7:00pm SRV Puja
5/3 Sun   9:30am Class: Teachings of Lord Buddha

SRV Oregon (Call for meditation times)
5/8 Fri   7:00pm Satsang with Babaji
5/9 Sat   9:30am Class: Teachings of Lord Buddha
           6:00pm SRV Puja, Siva Puja
5/10 Sun   9:30am Class: Upanisad
5/13 Wed   7:00pm Principles of the Upanisads, with Anurag
5/16 Sat   9:30am Class: Upanisad
           6:00pm SRV Puja, Siva Puja (Phalaharini)
5/17 Sun   9:30am Class: Upanisad
5/20 Wed   7:00pm Vedanta 101 with Annapurna Sarada
5/21 - 25 — SRV Spring Retreat

Memorial Day Weekend Retreat — 5/21 - 25
Subject: Manas-asana, The Art of Mental Postures
Location: Windwood Waters (Wind River Region)
(arrive Thursday evening, depart Monday at noon)

July, 2015

SRV San Francisco (Meditation, 6 to 7 am)
7/17 Fri   SRV SF Summer Retreat Begins

SRV American River Retreat over Gurupurnima
July 17th, eve - July 23rd, noon.   Forest Hill, Ca.

SRV Oregon (Call for meditation times)
7/31 Fri   7:00am Satsang with Babaji
8/1 Sat   9:30am Class: Upanisads
           6:00pm **Gurupurnima Puja**
8/2 Sun   9:30am Class: Upanisads
8/5 Wed   7:00pm Principles of the Upanisads, with Anurag
8/7 Fri   6:00 pm Satsang with Babaji
8/8 Sat   9:30 am Class: Upanisads
           6:00pm SRV Puja, Siva Puja
8/9 Sun   9:30 am Class: Upanisads
8/12 Wed   7:00pm Vedanta 101, with Annapurna Sarada
8/14-16 – SRV Weekend Seminar with Satsang
Subject: The Samadhis of Yoga
with Friday Satsang at 7 pm, & 2 classes Sat., 2 classes Sun.

October, 2015

SRV San Francisco (Meditation, 6 to 7 am)
10/9 Fri   7:00pm Arati/Satsang
10/10 Sat   9:30am Class: TBA
            7:00pm **Durga Puja**
10/11 Sun   9:30am Class: TBA

SRV Oregon (Call for meditation times)
10/16 Fri   7:00pm Satsang with Babaji
10/17 S at 9:30am Class: TBA
            6:00pm **Durga Puja**
10/18 Sun   9:30am Class: TBA
10/21 Wed   7:00pm Principles of the Upanisads, with Anurag
10/22 - 10/26 — SRV Fall Retreat

SRV Kali Durga Lakshmi Retreat
Location TBA – October 22nd - 26th
United Nations Day Weekend
Subject: Shaktadvaitavada & Kundalini Yoga

10/28 Wed 7:00pm Vedanta 101, with Annapurna Sarada
10/31 Sat   9:30am Class: TBA
            6:00pm SRV Puja, Siva Puja
11/1 Sun   9:30pm Class: TBA

Visit srv.org for all retreat details
Weekend Classes webcasted, 9:30 am to 12:30 pm, PST

---

* Vedanta for Teens & Children
at SRV Oregon and SRV San Francisco
Contact Annapurna Sarada — Ph: 808-990-3354

SRV Associations — Babaji's Teaching Schedule, 2015
SRV Hawaii Ashram, Big Island

Sunday Live Streaming Classes, 2:30 - 5:30pm
Hawaii SRV Ashram   Directions: Call: 808-990-3354

- **Neutralizing Karma and Samskaras**
  January 11, 25, & Feb 1, 2015
- **Success & Failure in Spiritual Life**
  March 22, 29, & April 5, 12, 19
- **Food, Prana, & Sadhana**
  June 7, 14, 21, 28, & July 5
- **Spandas: Cosmic Principles of Saivism**
  August 30, & September 6, 13, 20, 27
- **Topic: TBA**
  November 15, 22, 29, & Dec. 6, 13, 20, 27

**Annual Hawaii Retreat
over Martin Luther King Weekend**
Location: Puna, Big Island of Hawaii
Making Crucial Spiritual Connections II
January 15-18, 2016

Notice:
Our 2015 schedule is subject to change.
Please check the calendar on our website
www.srv.org
and sign our e-list at classes for notifications
or read our e-newsletter, Mundamala.
You can also contact your local SRV center:
Hawaii & Oregon: 808-990-3354
San Francisco: 415-468-4680

Check www.srv.org for Hawaii retreats
or see our Retreats Pages in the back of this issue

Sign up for:
- SRV Magazine: Nectar of Non-Dual Truth
- Raja Yoga email study with Babaji
- SRV's Facebook page

* Please call or inquire about our Children's Classes
Contact Annapurna Sarada — Phone 808-990-3354

SRV Hawai'i Administrative Office:	SRV Associations' website:
PO Box 1364 Honoka'a, HI 96727 Ph: 808-990-3354	www.srv.org email: srvinfo@srv.org

See our SRV Facebook Page   facebook.com/srv.vedanta

SRV Associations Website
www.srv.org
srvinfo@srv.org

SRV On The Web
Visit www.srv.org to find:

SRV's Livestream Channel
Webcast Time Zone Schedule
SRV's YouTube Channel Class Series
- Advaita of the Avatars
- Devotion of Nonseparation
- The Wisdom Particle
- Non-Touch Yoga
- Shakta-Advaita-vada

Explore our Website links to find:
- Sanskrit Chants to learn/practice
- Devotional Songs
- Audio Discourses

Teachings:
- Articles
- Raja Yoga Sutras Study
- SRV's Teachings for Youth/Children
- Podcasts

Magazine:
- View our online archive of Nectar
- Order back issues of Nectar

News & Events
- Mundamala – SRV's e-newsletter
  Full of teachings and more

SRV Associations — Retreats for 2015

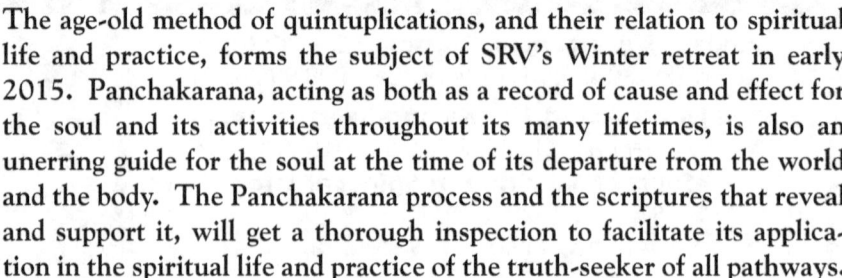

SRV Winter Retreat
February 26 – March 2nd, 2015, Seattle, Washington
Retreat Topic: Panchadasi & Panchakarana

The age-old method of quintuplications, and their relation to spiritual life and practice, forms the subject of SRV's Winter retreat in early 2015. Panchakarana, acting as both as a record of cause and effect for the soul and its activities throughout its many lifetimes, is also an unerring guide for the soul at the time of its departure from the world and the body. The Panchakarana process and the scriptures that reveal and support it, will get a thorough inspection to facilitate its application in the spiritual life and practice of the truth-seeker of all pathways.

"The illumined seer who revealed this essential wisdom by his deep intuition, having grouped the various elements of existence, declared that the entire universe of gross and subtle worlds is based in sets of fivefold principles, and that one set of fives enables and preserves the next set of fives. The seer opens up cosmic vision by knowing this principle of fives based on facts known to all."

Taittiriya Upanisad

Text: *Panchadasi & Taittiriya Upanisad*   **Location:** Seattle, Washington
Arrival: Thursday, February 26, after dinner and by 10:00pm   **Departure:** Monday, March 2nd, at 12:00pm
Tuition (all inclusive): $300; students $150   **Registration:** Starts now. Tuition is due by Feb 11th
Financial hardship?   Call 808-990-3354   **Register by email:** srvinfo@srv.org or by phone 808-990-3354

SRV Spring Retreat Over Memorial Day
May 21 – 25th, 2015, Wind River region, Washington
Subject: The Spiritual Art of Mental Posture

The most beneficial usage of an asana is mental, not physical. As the scriptures of India declare, *"Not by hundreds and thousands of body postures, but by control of the mind, does the soul reach Enlightenment."*

In SRV's Spring retreat at Windwood Waters near the Columbia River Gorge in Washington state, participants and practitioners of all ages will learn about the wealth of mental postures that the mind can adopt, as well as how to apply them in order to render the soul balanced and peaceful and gain that everlasting state of yogic equilibrium that is conducive to Self-realization in this life.

Location: Windwood Waters retreat site near Stevenson, WA
Arrival: Thursday, May 21, between 4:00 & 9:00 pm
Departure: Monday, May 25, 1:00pm
Registration: Starts now. Tuition and lodging fees are due by May 7th
Register by email: srvinfo@srv.org or by phone 808-990-3354
Costs: Tuition and meals: $390; Students:: $205 (lodging additional)
Lodging: private room single, $240; private room shared with 1 - 2 others, $160/person; semi-private lodge sleeping, $120*; Tenting, $80*
*bring your own bedding/towels

SRV American River Retreat, 2015
July 17 – 23, 2015, Forest Hill, CA
- **Select Teachings of the Dharma for all Age Groups**
- Live in holy company for a full week – meditating, studying, serving, and growing together.
- Each morning begins with chanting from the Bhagavad Gita prior to meditation.
- Daily classes include essential teachings of Yoga, Vedanta, Tantra, and Sankhya.
- Afternoons include explorations and swimming/sunning along the American River.
- Afternoon Chela Dharma class for teens and young adults.
- Evening devotions at the altar, singing and chanting, meditation, and satsang.
- Concurrent Children's Retreat — Children, ages 6 to approximately 13 have their own simultaneous retreat. Activities include "salute to the sun," morning ritual, meditation, Vedic stories and lessons, and arts and crafts.

Location: Private land in Foresthill, California near the American River
Arrival: Arrive by 6pm, Friday evening, July 17th
Last day of retreat: Wednesday, July 23 (approximately noon, clean up follows)
Tuition: all inclusive
   Adults: $610 (full retreat) $275 (weekend, arrive Friday) $110/day
   Children/Students: $305 (full retreat) $140 (weekend, arrive Friday) $55/day
Registration: starts now and tuition is due by Friday, July 3rd
Financial hardship? Call 808-990-3354 to discuss options
Register by email: srvinfo@srv.org or by phone 808-990-3354

"Then, the hoary old rishi, Lord Vasishtha, told the young Sri Ram: 'They attain to the Supreme Self who study the Atma-jnan scriptures with an able preceptor from their early youth.'"

Autumn Retreat Concluding Navaratri
October 22 – 26th, 2015, Location: To Be Announced
Subject: The Profound Teachings and Secrets of the Divine Mother Path

This powerful retreat at the end of holy Navaratri in October will focus in on the many teachings of the Shaktadvaita pathway, combining them naturally with the salient disciplines of Kundalini Yoga.

Location: TBA
Arrival: Thursday, October 22 after 6:00pm
Departure: Monday, October 26, 12:00pm
Tuition & Meals: Adults: $410: Student: $225 (lodging additional)
Lodging: Private room single, $240; Private room shared, $160/person
semi-private lodge sleeping, $120; tenting, $80 bring your own bedding/towels
Registration: Starts now. Tuition and other fees are due by October 8th

---

Plus: Two SRV Seminars in 2015

How a Householder Renounces the World
Location: SRV Oregon Ashram in Portland
Saturday, March 7: 6:00am – 5:00pm (breakfast/dinner)
Sunday, March 8: 6:00am – 12:00pm (breakfast only)
Tuition: $165; student, $95

The Samadhis of Yoga
Location: SRV Oregon Ashram in Portland
Friday, August 14: 7:00 PM – Satsang
Saturday, August 15: 6:00am – 5:00pm (breakfast/dinner)
Sunday, August 16: 6:00am – 5:00pm (breakfast only)
Tuition: $230; student, $125

Accommodations: These are non-residential seminars
Contact us if you would like assistance with lodging. 808-990-3354 // srvinfo@srv.org

"The monk must renounce inwardly and outwardly. The householder must renounce only inwardly." Sri Ramakrishna

The "In The Spirit" Interviews of Lex Hixon

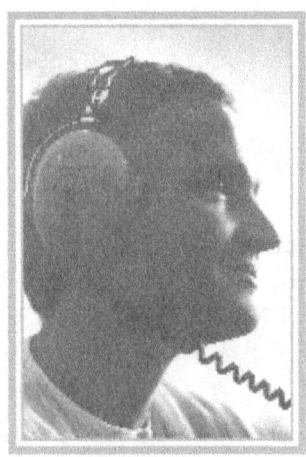

Lex Hixon

From the early 1970's on through the late 1980's, Lex Hixon hosted a radio program in New York City that was unprecedented in its depth, scope, insight and unique creativity. First entitled "In The Spirit," it also later appeared under the titles of "Body/Mind/Spirit," and "Spirit/Mind/Body."

On this long running inspirational program that spanned over two decades and which was duly sponsored in listener-supported fashion on WBAI Radio, Lex interviewed educators, healers, clergy, authors, artists, psychics, spiritual leaders and others.

As a list, the fruit of this selfless work reads like a comprehensive Who's Who of the spiritual, artistic and intellectual heart and mind of both Eastern and Western cultures. With subtle tenderness and insight, though never lacking the penetrating edge which makes for excellent broadcasting, Lex welcomed the orthodox and the unorthodox, the conservative and the radical, the famous and the obscure, the popular and the controversial, the powerful and the humble, the aggressive and the retiring.

Included in this copious series are interviews with gurus, yogis, swamis, priests, roshis, rabbis/rebbes, sheikhs, lamas, rinpoches, poets, musicians, psychics, occultists, authors, writers, teachers, politicians, businessmen and more.

- Over 325 Titles to choose from
- Individual CD's are available
- Trio sets
- Full set prices
- List of all titles available upon request
- Highest quality materials used

"IN THE SPIRIT" CD Trio Sets
Choice selections from the cassette series on CD

Buddhist
B1 - Tibetan
Dalai Lama
Kalu Rinpoche
Trungpa Rinpoche

B2 - Zen
Eido Roshi
Soen Roshi
Maesumi Roshi

B3 - American
Phillip Kapleau
Bernie Glassman
Robert Thurman

Christianity
C1 - Mother Teresa
Padre Pio
Meister Ekhart

Islam/Sufism
IS1 - Sheikh Muzaffer
Guru Bawa
Sheikh Nur Al Jerrahi

Judaism
J1 - Rabbi Shlomo Carlebach
Rebbe Gedalia
Rabbi Zalman Schachter

J2 - Rebbi Meyer Fund
Rabbi Dovid Din
Rabbi Lynn Gotleib

Lex Hixon
H1 - On the Haj
On the Karmapa
On Himself

Professors & Authors
PA1 - Huston Smith
Christopher Isherwood
Jack Cornfield

PA2 - David Spangler
Alan Watts
Alan Ginsberg

Shamanism/Amer. Indian
SI1 - Oh Shinnah
Dhani Thorna
Don Juan

Vedic
V1 - Sri Ramakrishna

V2 - Ramakrishna Order Swamis
Vivekananda
Nikhilananda
Prabhavananda

V3 - Swamis
Dayananda
Muktananda
Satchitananda

V4 - Special Luminaries
Ramana Maharshi
Sri Aurobindo
Krishnamurti

V5 - Spiritual Teachers
Meher Baba
Sri Chinmoy
Ram Das

V6 - Divine Mother of the Universe

Postal Orders: Jai Ma Music, PO Box 380, Paauilo, HI 96776
Email Orders: srvinfo@srv.org
Phone Orders: 808-990-3354
Website: www.srv.org

Advaita-satya-amritam

NECTAR
of Non-Dual Truth

Donation/Order Form
Suggested donation $12 *per issue*

Nectar #31 is available for free if you write, email, or call for a copy before Feb. 1st, 2016
Your generous donations make Nectar available to others and help us to widen our distribution.

Those who donate $12 *or more for the next issue, will be added to our subscriber's list.*
- ❏ Please send me/my triend a free copy of the next issue of Nectar.
- ❏ Send me ___ copies to give to friends or a spiritual center of my choice.
- ❏ I am enclosing the names of persons/centers I want to receive Nectar. *Fill out the back of this form.*

- ❏ I want to help SRV's free Nectar distribution program ($50 and up)
- ❏ I want to help widen Nectar's distribution ($200 and up)
- ❏ I want to make sure there are future issues of Nectar ($500 and up)

Please fill out the back side of this form and mail it with your check to:
SRV Associations, PO Box 1364, Honokaa, HI 96727
MasterCard or Visa accepted ♦ Make checks payable to: SRV Associations
808-990-3354 ♦ srvinfo@srv.org ♦ www.srv.org

#30

Advaita-satya-amritam

NECTAR
of Non-Dual Truth

Donation/Order Form
Suggested donation $12 *per issue*

Nectar #31 is available for free if you write, email, or call for a copy before Feb. 1st, 2016
Your generous donations make Nectar available to others and help us to widen our distribution.

Those who donate $12 *or more for the next issue, will be added to our subscriber's list.*
- ❏ Please send me/my triend a free copy of the next issue of Nectar.
- ❏ Send me ___ copies to give to friends or a spiritual center of my choice.
- ❏ I am enclosing the names of persons/centers I want to receive Nectar. *Fill out the back of this form.*

- ❏ I want to help SRV's free Nectar distribution program ($50 and up)
- ❏ I want to help widen Nectar's distribution ($200 and up)
- ❏ I want to make sure there are future issues of Nectar ($500 and up)

Please fill out the back side of this form and mail it with your check to:
SRV Associations, PO Box 1364, Honokaa, HI 96727
MasterCard or Visa accepted ♦ Make checks payable to: SRV Associations
808-990-3354 ♦ srvinfo@srv.org ♦ www.srv.org

#30

Advaita-satya-amritam

NECTAR
of Non-Dual Truth

Donation/Order Form
Suggested donation $12 *per issue*

Nectar #31 is available for free if you write, email, or call for a copy before Feb. 1st, 2016
Your generous donations make Nectar available to others and help us to widen our distribution.

Those who donate $12 *or more for the next issue, will be added to our subscriber's list.*
- ❏ Please send me/my triend a free copy of the next issue of Nectar.
- ❏ Send me ___ copies to give to friends or a spiritual center of my choice.
- ❏ I am enclosing the names of persons/centers I want to receive Nectar. *Fill out the back of this form.*

- ❏ I want to help SRV's free Nectar distribution program ($50 and up)
- ❏ I want to help widen Nectar's distribution ($200 and up)
- ❏ I want to make sure there are future issues of Nectar ($500 and up)

Please fill out the back side of this form and mail it with your check to:
SRV Associations, PO Box 1364, Honokaa, HI 96727
MasterCard or Visa accepted ♦ Make checks payable to: SRV Associations
808-990-3354 ♦ srvinfo@srv.org ♦ www.srv.org

#30

Your Information:

Name: _____

Address: _____

City, State, Zip: _____

Email: _____

Additional Address: (please use a sheet of paper for more addresses)

Name: _____

Address: _____

City, State, Zip: _____

Email: _____

Do you wish to pay by Mastercard or Visa?

Card No.: _____ **Amount:** _____

Exp. date: _____ **Phone no.:** _____

Signature: _____

Questions? call SRV Associations: 808-990-3354

Your Information:

Name: _____

Address: _____

City, State, Zip: _____

Email: _____

Additional Address: (please use a sheet of paper for more addresses)

Name: _____

Address: _____

City, State, Zip: _____

Email: _____

Do you wish to pay by Mastercard or Visa?

Card No.: _____ **Amount:** _____

Exp. date: _____ **Phone no.:** _____

Signature: _____

Questions? call SRV Associations: 808-990-3354

Your Information:

Name: _____

Address: _____

City, State, Zip: _____

Email: _____

Additional Address: (please use a sheet of paper for more addresses)

Name: _____

Address: _____

City, State, Zip: _____

Email: _____

Do you wish to pay by Mastercard or Visa?

Card No.: _____ **Amount:** _____

Exp. date: _____ **Phone no.:** _____

Signature: _____

Questions? call SRV Associations: 808-990-3354

www.ingramcontent.com/pod-product-compliance
Lightning Source LLC
Chambersburg PA
CBHW081127080526
44587CB00021B/3781